Dr. Tom Tufts, January, 2014

Dear Friend,

Welcome to a life-changing journey. I am excited that you have chosen to embark on this adventure. And, I can promise you, that it will be a challenging move from where you are today to where God wants and needs you to be tomorrow.

This is a journey filled with small, incremental steps. You really can't run until you have crawled. So it's important that you don't skip any of the steps in the process.

There may be times that you may feel that the information is a bit juvenile or that you have already accomplished the growth step at hand. My advice would be evaluate the information and **_make sure_** that you are ready to proceed.

These texts are not intended to help you walk. They are not designed to help you run. The dream is that by the end you can *fly*. *So many people today, even those in the faith, are living self-deprecating, defeated, miniscule lives when God has so much more in store for us. Let's live like the champions that He designed, created, equipped and desires that we can be! Let's live life, to the hilt, ON PURPOSE.*

Each text in this series will begin with the same requirement. Answer this one simple question:

What is your purpose in life?

Is it to make as much money as possible? Is it to sell everything you have and help the poor? Is it to discover the cure for cancer?

What is YOUR purpose?

Here's why this is important: Putting this objective into one, simple sentence, will help you *focus on what is critically important and intentional, and ignore that which is not important and is distracting.*

There are many good things in our lives. (Hobbies, careers, possessions, family, vacations, and many more). These things are valuable. These things are part of our everyday lives. These things are *good things*. But if we are not careful, the "good things" can keep us from the *"great things."*

I have yet to meet someone who sets out to be a failure. Everyone I have ever met desires and intends to be a shining star, to be a great success. What I have learned is that a) success doesn't happen by accident and that b) failure does not happen by accident, either.

If you want to fulfil your life's purpose, you are going to have to a) state it clearly b) focus on pursuing it c) limit the distractions and d) purge your life of the obstacles.

You have to choose to *intentionally succeed in every area of life.* Keep in mind that YOUR PURPOSE (different than mine) is the **same** while the **behaviours learned** in each area of life are different.

My wife and I share a purpose: To share laughter and the joy of Christ, while touching six continents (NOT ANTARTICA!) leaving a ministry and legacy of health, faithfulness and the Christian faith all over the world, and especially to our family.

My **personal purpose** is a bit different **but it does not contradict my marital purpose:**

I am intentionally focused on becoming an relationally, financially, and physically healthy husband, father and grandfather, serving my family and friends through my daily actions, while modelling the life of Christ and the Kingdom of God, while laughing and enjoying the entire journey.

Stating what you are about brings specific focus to your life. It allows you to say 'yes' and 'no' to events, situations and people in your life. It eliminates the worry, stress and guilt of finding

FINANCIAL HEALTH: ON PURPOSE

IF IT'S IMPORTANT, IT'S INTENTIONAL.

Dr. Tom Tufts

FRIENDS MEDIA GROUP

Friends Media Group

FINANCIAL HEALTH ON PURPOSE

TABLE OF CONTENTS

Meet Stuart	8
How Do You Define Stewardship?	24
It's Not Up To Us	28
Is Stewardship Really All That Important?	32
What Is The Right Amount To Give?	36
What's Right, or What's Left?	48
Giving Until It Hurts	52
Learning How To Give Cheerfully	65
What Belongs To Me?	70
Just Exactly What Is a Tithe?	74
Multiple Tithes Hurt	80
Is Tithing For the Modern Day Believer?	84

direction. It speeds up the decision making process and streamlines your life.

I have yet to meet anyone, anywhere that has experienced significant life change without doing two things:
1. They make *dramatic, daily **changes** to their behaviour.*
2. *They do these things **intentionally** because they have their eyes on the goal.*

In 1982, Tom Watson and Jack Nicklaus were locked in a tussle for one of golf's 'major' tournaments. Nicklaus had played great and tied Watson on this final day and finished about 45 minutes earlier.

On the par three, 17th hole, golf history was made. Watson hit his tee shot, and pulled it to the left. In golf they say "every shot makes somebody happy." I would guess that at this moment Nicklaus, watching TV from the clubhouse, was feeling a bit relieved. After hitting the shot, Watson shook his head in disgust. He knew how thick the grass was. He knew what he was up against.

Watson faced a very difficult shot. His chances of making a '3' were almost impossible.

If you are unfamiliar with golf let me try to describe the moment to you.

The golf ball was not very far from the hole, maybe only thirty feet. However, it was in some very deep grass. In fact, it was in so deep that you couldn't see the ball from the TV camera. Come to think of it, you could barely see Tom Watson's *shoes*.

Watson's caddie, Bruce Edwards, said, "Get it close." Watson gave one of the great responses of all time: "Close? I'm going to make it."

Tom Watson didn't get it close. Watson popped the ball up in the air, and it dropped in the cup for a 'birdie' and a one shot lead over Jack Nicklaus.

That's right. Tom Watson chipped in on the 71st hole of the US Open at Pebble Beach to take a one shot lead. I remember watching it 'live' on TV when it happened. I was sick to my stomach.

With a one-stroke lead (his purpose completed) he went on to birdie the 18th hole for a ***two-stroke*** victory. (Very few people talk about the fact that even with a par, his birdie on 18 would have sealed the victory. Nicklaus has called this the most painful defeat in his entire career).

In the press conference Watson was asked about the miracle shot. It was referred to as having 'divine influence.' It was called a 'once in a lifetime shot.'

Watson said, "Yes, it was the greatest shot of my career. It's amazing how, the more I practice, the luckier I get."

You can bet that Tom Watson had practiced 'that shot,' and tens of thousands *like it,* before. Every kid growing up practices thinking, "This is to win the US Open." In fact, I would guess that he practiced shots *in even worse situations than that one.* **And because he was prepared (focused and intentional) he was able to pull off the behaviour and fulfil his purpose.**

Now it's your turn to move beyond the mediocrity and experience life like God designed: full of joy, peace, health, growth, maturity, and for you to *<u>thrive.</u>* Let's get on with the journey!

What is your purpose?
Write it here:

(You may have to write it out, several times, on another sheet of paper).
If you are married, what is your marital purpose?
Write it here:

(You may have to write it out, several times, on another sheet of paper).

In the *NEXT book* you will be able to write it out by heart.

If It's Important, It's Intentional.
That's living life *ON PURPOSE.*

Meet Stuart

In recent months, I have been drawn to this simple phrase: "Living life On Purpose. If it's important, it's got to be intentional." I don't know where it came from or how it came to me. But in reality, there's nothing about your life or my life that's of any great value that we don't do on purpose, intentionally. And if that's true, (and I am pretty sure it is) then that is how I want to live. And, for those who look to me for leadership or influence, that's how I want to lead.

In this book we will look extensively on what the Bible teaches about finances. And continue to ask the question, "How do we intentionally create and operate by means of "Healthy Finances On Purpose?"

Imagine this past January. For many people it means that it is just a couple of weeks passed Christmas. Oh the memories. But it also means a visit from the Grinch, which for many people this means that Bill is coming to see us. And "Bill" may be disguised as Visa, Mastercard, Discover, or American Express. But either way, there's a bill coming.

And now some of us are wondering, "How do we pay for Christmas?" Or, "What happens when I'm over extended? What happens when I'm not understanding what happens with my income and my outgo?"

For many, many years of my own life, our married life together, we lived without an "official budget." I can tell you from personal experience that until you sit down and put things into a budget -this comes in; this goes out- it's hard to ever get ahead. I would venture to say it's impossible to move forward.

You need to answer this question, even before we get started. What is your purpose? I'm not asking what your goal for this year. I'm not asking you to name a goal for your life. Instead: What is your purpose?

In other words, when the minister stands there, at the end of your time, and they get up and say, "So-and-so completed their job. They finished the race," as the Scriptures say. They've finished all they were supposed to do. What would be said about you?

What is your purpose? Why are you here? "I'm here to make a million dollars." Well, in your lifetime, you probably will make a million. You probably will. If you make $20,000 per year and you work for 50 years, that's a million. It doesn't matter how you get there, that's a million. My question is, what's your purpose? When we get to the end of the road, do we want to be able to say, "Well they made 10 million dollars in their life, but they were an absolute loser." I don't think that's what you want said about you or a loved one.

So what is your purpose, what do you want people to say about you? What you're going to have to do is sit down with a piece of paper and you're going to have to wrestle with this, over and over again. And you want to put it in one sentence. It's not a paragraph.

This is my purpose. Right here. So that every decision I make, if it's not on purpose, then you decide 'no' because a "boundary" is saying 'no' to one thing so you can say 'yes' to something else. So I say 'no' to that, so I can accomplish my purpose.

Your purpose should not contradict the purpose you have for your family. This is my purpose. This is not my wife and my purpose. This is *my* purpose. Ours together will be very similar, and it will dovetail with my personal purpose.

My purpose is "to have a lot of fun influencing people toward the Kingdom." That's my purpose. My purpose is not to sell insurance. I did that. My purpose is not to be a golf pro. I did that. *Those professions are not my purpose.*

> *"My purpose is to have a lot of fun influencing people toward the Kingdom and to leave a legacy to my family of passionate faith and a legacy of being emotionally, physically, socially, and spiritually healthy."*

That's my purpose. Everything else is fluff to me. That's my purpose.

Now when Sherry and I sit down and say our purpose together, our purpose together is different but very similar to this and should not contradict this. So what's your purpose? What's your family's purpose? Knowing it, being able to recite it, allows you to say 'yes' and 'no' to things that are distractions. Sit down, come up with your purpose, because you really do need to know what your purpose is.

In sales, they call it an elevator speech. It's when you get in an elevator and you've got four floors to talk to someone. And they say, "What do you do?" And you say to them, "Well, my purpose is to have a whole lot of fun influencing people toward the Kingdom of God and leaving behind a legacy of spiritual maturity, faith, etc." And they respond, "Whaaaa?"

That's what you want! You've got to know your purpose and it's got to be so real and so right there at the surface that it drives and guides everything that you do. Every area of life. Including your finances.

I want to introduce you to my friend Stewart. Stewart owns a really, really, really, really big boat. In fact some people say the boat is so big, it's called a ship. Now I don't think ships are ever called boats. But I do think that at some point, a boat can become a ship. Just depends on how big it is. And my friend Stewart, he owns a really, really big boat.

Everything you can ever imagine is on this boat. Anything. It doesn't matter what you can picture in your mind, you can find it on this boat. That's how big the boat is. Stewart owns a boat and on the boat there's everything.

*Anybody **can** get on the boat.* Anybody. You're welcome to ride on the boat. "Come on, ride on my boat!" That's what Stewart would say. "Come on, ride on my boat." However, Stewart has some guidelines about people getting on the boat. For example, Stewart might want you to be able to swim. That would make some sense, right? You've got to be able to swim.

Stewart could say, "Only left-handed people can get on the boat." Because it's Stewarts boat and he can do what he wants, would you agree? So anybody can get on the boat, but *some people choose not to get on the boat.* And they choose to have their own boat instead. Stewart has a boat. But they want to drive their own boat. They don't want to be a passenger on Stewart's boat, so they choose to stay on their own boat. Because Stewart has certain guidelines and they don't want to learn how to swim. And they're right-handed. So they don't ever get on Stewart's boat. Stewart doesn't understand that, because Stewart's perspective is, "I've got everything on the boat. Why wouldn't you want to get on my boat?" Their answer is simple: "Because I'd rather drive my own."

Here is the strange part: Stewart will let you and other people drive their own boat. In order to ride on his boat, you have to acknowledge that you don't have a boat and that his is superior to all of the other boats.

Can you imagine the day that Stewart, the owner of the really big boat with everything, comes to you and says, "Here are the keys. You are now captain of the boat." You're like, "This is awesome! I get to drive the boat."

Well, driving the boat is only part of it. You have to take care of the boat. Everything on the boat. Every person on the boat. You've got to keep it fueled, you've got to keep it clean. You've got to feed everybody. Now you can have fun with everything that's on the boat! You can barbecue, you can go to the pool, you can do the little surfing thing on the tidal wave, whatever-that-is. You can do whatever you want on the boat.

But, you have to take care of the boat. Because sooner or later, Stewart is going to come back to get the boat. Stewart is going to sit down with you, the captain, and he's going to say, "Hey, I gave you the keys to the boat. What did you do with the boat? I notice over here, there's a bunch of broken windows. You were supposed to fix the windows." You wonder why the windows are broken and then it dawns on you. "Oh, wait, I was the captain of the boat!" You remember, Stewart has put you in charge of the boat.

Now on the boat, you can use just about anything you want... except a small portion. You can only use 90%. You can't really use *all* the boat. You can only use 90% of the boat.

You say, "Well, why is that?" That's because there's a room. It's just one room. It's a little room, a little tiny room. It's about 10% of the boat and you can't use it because *that's where Stewart keeps his money. And that's his money.* It's not your money. And you and I cannot use Stewart's money to do what we want.

Because the captain is eventually going to come back and say, "I counted my money and there's money missing. You, Mr. Captain, are responsible, even if that guy stole it, you are responsible because I put you in charge of the ship." So you see, you can use almost all of the ship, but not quite all of it.

Can you imagine if a wealthy person gave you 25% of their wealth? You'd say, "Wow!" And if a really, really wealthy person gave you 80% of their wealth, you'd say, "This is incredible!" God's giving you 90%. **Of all the resources you get, you get 90%.** All Stewart's asking for is 10%. And in that room where Stewart keeps his money, we're not to use Stewart's money to do our thing -maintaining the boat- because Stewart himself will ask the people who are the caretakers, "Where's my stuff?"

The *reason* you take care of the boat is *because you appreciate Stewart* being nice to you, letting you on the boat, and *because you appreciate Stewart* handing you the keys to the boat, *because you appreciate Stewart* letting you use 90% of the boat. You are willing to do anything to protect his boat. *Anything.* Against pirates, against anybody who would attack, even against crewmen! You will do whatever it takes, *because you value Stewart,* to protect his boat. You'll get down on your own hands and knees and scrub that deck. You'll make sure that there's no damage to that boat. And when Stewart comes back, you and I were taught as kids, that when you return something, it's in as good or better condition as when you got it. And when Stewart comes back, you want to look good. After all, it is... *Stewart's ship.*

It's not a perfect analogy. But that's stewardship. That is what stewardship is. God says, "It's my boat. Do what you want with it. 90% of it. But that little room on the boat.. you don't go in there, you don't use it." In the book of Malachi it says because when we do and we use God's money, we 'rob' Him. That's what it says. It's Stewart's ship.

And this is what stewardship is all about. It's not about money. It's about "taking care of." It's about "looking after." Your children are not yours. They're only yours to look after. They are not yours. And the day that they learn to walk and you held them up and they stumbled that first step, that is the first step *away from you.* They're not your kids. They're His kids.

Anything that you can see on the boat, anything that you can imagine, seen or unseen, the Bible says, is Stewart's. Not ours. Whatever you can taste, whatever you can touch, whatever you can taste, it is not yours. It belongs to God. It does not belong to us. *Stewardship is based upon appreciation.*

Pastors and churches are afraid to talk about two things: Evangelism and Stewardship. But they go together. Stewardship is not about money, it's not about tithing, it's not about dollars, it's not about any of that. Stewardship is about appreciation. And if you don't appreciate Stewart letting you on the boat, if you don't appreciate this amazing grace, then you don't protect the ship. You don't guard it. But if you do appreciate it, stewardship is a natural out flowing of who we are and how we care. How we feel about God, for God's people, and for *God's purpose. Stewardship is a heart issue, not a finances issue. Stewardship is something that you demonstrate, not talk about.*

Let me give you an example. Remember as we were growing up, those of us who grew up in the 60's, 70's and 80's, our Moms and Dads went and bought a house. My Mom and Dad's first house was $37,000. Their house payment was $104. I remember it well. But for my Mom and Dad, that house (1738 Kaiser Drive, Reynoldsburg, OH) was the most extravagant thing they could have ever bought... a house.

As you grow up, you're living there, but it's *their house*. And when you're little, you break things. I broke a screen door. I fell through a dining room window. I was leaning back in my chair like you aren't supposed to. Note to self: don't do that again!

And when it's not your house, and something breaks, the tendency is to think, "What's the big deal?"

But then all of a sudden, you become 40 and you own the house, and it's a big deal isn't it? It's a big deal when your kid gets mad and puts their fist through the dry wall. That's a big deal. Because that's *your* house.

Now here's the thing, when you're little, you don't understand. As adults, we get it. You just don't understand. But when you grow older, it should bother you. It should bother us when we break something that belongs to someone else. But, it's not our house, not our problem.

The thought (or maturity) is, "It's Mom and Dad's house. It's their stuff. And I should keep care of it. And if I appreciate it, I'll take care of it." That's why, as we get older, and those of us who are adult children who still have living parents, we're still afraid to death to use their stuff. Because we don't want it to break.

The thing is, this is an American problem. *It really doesn't matter what we think about something. It matters what the Bible says.* It doesn't matter, our opinion. "Well, what do you think about this issue?" It doesn't matter what I think. It matters what the Bible says. And if we're going to live our life "On Purpose", we've got to understand what God's purpose is and God's purpose is written for us to live out according to His word. What that means is, what I think about what's going on socially, what I think about what's going on politically, what I think about what's going on in the world economically, it doesn't matter. What matters is what the Bible says about it.

When I was buying a house, we had two criteria. We really wanted a house that had a pool, or we wanted to buy a house on a lake, and the reason is because with Lucas (our grandson) growing up, we wanted to have a really good excuse for him to come see Mimi and Doc. So that's why we have a house with a pool.

No One Will Take Care of Your Pool Like You Will

I was speaking to my realtor and I said I thought I'd get a pool service and she said, "No one will take care of your pool like you will." And she's right. No one's going to take care of your stuff like you take care of your stuff.

Some of you men, your tools are like gold to you. And nobody puts them back like you do. Some of us, it's our computer, our clothes, whatever it is, nobody will take as care of it as well as you will.

This is a favorite Scripture: "Train up a child in the way that they will go and when they're old, they will never depart from it." [Proverbs 2:6] Keep in mind, it's a principle, not a promise. It's a principle. Chances are, if you raise them the right way, they'll stick with the right way. Or at least come back to the right way. That's a principle.

Have you ever looked at *the next verse?* Here's what the next verse says. Maybe this is something we should teach our kids... Proverbs 22:7 "Just as the rich rule the poor, the borrower is servant to the lender." The borrower is subject to the owner.

A few years ago, there was a thing called adjustable rate mortgages. The current interest rate on the mortgage was attached to the value of the dollar. And some folks refinanced their houses and said things like "I got a low 3.8%" and then over time, the rate when sky high because and ARM can keep going up. *And the lender can tell you, at any moment, that your rate just went up.* That means your house payment went up. That's what an adjustable rate is. They adjust it up and down, up and down. It's an adjustable rate and *you never know what you're going to get.* These were very popular. **But it was the lender who was in charge.**

Rental cars are a really good example of this principle. Most people treat a rental car much differently than they treat their own car. We leave trash in them, we throw stuff on the floor, spill ketchup on the seats and 'try' to wipe it up with a wet wipe. Oh well. After all, my last name isn't "Hertz". I don't care. I don't have to care about this car. You race it, your drive it different, you slam on the brakes. Why? Because you borrowed it for a couple of days and you're going to turn it back in. And if it gets messed up, who cares? You don't have to drive it again, right? See here's the problem. *It's human nature to just overlook taking care of things that aren't ours. It's not mine. It's not my problem. I'm going to use it and I'm going to get rid of it. I don't care. That's human nature.*

But here's the biblical perspective: *the spiritual nature trumps the human nature.* That's where this "problem" develops.

My spiritual side should be able to overrule my human side. If I'm walking with the Spirit of God, I can do all things. I can learn how to take care of things *that are not mine.* Nobody's going to take care of my pool like I am. So why would I trust it to somebody else? He has no investment in my pool. So I'm going to take care of my own pool. I'm going to have to learn how to do it. But he's still not going to take better care than I will because I have an investment in that pool.

And for us, stewardship is a matter of *maturity*. "I really appreciate this. I get it. Stewart let me on the boat. Because he was so kind to me, I'm going to look after his stuff. And I'm going to do what I can to help other people too." *That is stewardship.*

We have forgotten that we are overseers of God's stuff. We act like renters. Borrowers. When we're truly owners. "Heirs of the Kingdom" is what the Bible says. What that means is, what's His is eventually ours and what's His right now, we've been put in charge of. *We don't have to act like we're borrowing it. We have to act like we own it. And we take care of it. That's stewardship.* Taking care of God's stuff. Looking after the pool.

<u>Love is demonstrated by the amount of care that you give.</u>

In other words, let's say that we value relationships on a scale of 1 to 10. For a relationship that see as a 1, I'm most likely going to look after it differently than a relationship that I think is a 9. The people that are 9s to me, I really love and care about these people, I'm going to make sure I look after their stuff. Why? Because they mean a lot to me. Let me give you an example.

A few years ago, when Sherry and I lived in Michigan, we were going to come to Florida for the holidays. We didn't have a vehicle that we could all fit in, so my parents allowed me to borrow their car. My dad went and spent several hundred dollars to get his car tuned up and get it road ready for that trip. It's 1300 miles.

I drove it all the way to Florida, drove around down for ten days or so and drove it all the way back to Michigan. I'm pulling into my house, wife and kids in the car. I drive past my mailbox and I forgot something so I backed up. And when I did, the mailbox hit my Dad's side view mirror and broke it. I'd driven that joker 3,000 miles. I was next to my driveway. I have killed my Dad's car. So you know what I did? I went and got it fixed *before* I gave it to my Dad. Why? I didn't want my Dad to know I had damaged his car. Because I love my Dad. And I know my Dad loved that car. I didn't want to give it back to him broken. Because you know what he would have said to me? "Man, everything's in great shape. Everything except the side view mirror. How do you suppose that happened?" And then I would have told him what happened. "Some kid broke in my driveway, beat it with a ball bat, I don't know, Dad." That's what I would have said. But I took care of it. The next day. After driving from Atlanta all the way to Michigan in one day, I got up and went to the Buick dealer and sat there for hours while they fixed that mirror just so I could give it back to my Dad in good shape. Because I really, really love my Dad.

Not too long ago a friend of ours let us borrow their lake house. And at the lake house, there's a boat, a pontoon, and a jet ski. I used to have a boat, and I know how hard boats are to keep maintained. [If you don't know what a boat is, just dig a hole in the lake and throw money in it. It's about the same.] And I know how expensive boats are and I know that it's not even the boat but it's the engine that costs so much money. And these people have a dock. And you have to pull the boat in a certain way. I was afraid I was going to hit their dock and knock their dock over. And I'm afraid I'm going to go out and blow the engine up on this boat. And I'm going to go out on the jet ski and break my neck and have to sue them.

To make it worse, my adult children, 18 and 20 years old, use the jet ski and I'm thinking they're going to blow an engine and I'm going to be liable for this jet ski. I had real trouble just relaxing and it's because the folks that allowed me to go there... I really like them. I like them a lot. And I wanted to protect their stuff. And when we were done at their house, we cleaned their house. Why? Because you're supposed to. That's why. *Because I love them.* I love them a lot and what they did for me was a huge sacrifice. And I appreciated it.

That's stewardship. I'm looking after your stuff. And I'm treating it like my own. Even better than my own. Because it's yours. Nobody will watch your stuff like you will. But you love people by showing how much you appreciate what they've done for you. And when we care deeply, we love deeply. When you care, you do whatever it takes to show people that you love them. And there's nothing you would do that would violate that relationship.

It's a love condition. It's an indicator. If I don't look after God's stuff, it indicates I don't love Him very much. But if I really, really care for God and His things, then I show it by taking care of His stuff. That's what that shows. And ultimately stewardship is not a dollars issue, it's a heart issue. It's a heart problem. And it's an indication that I've got an issue. I could blame it on everybody else. It's my coach's fault, my teacher's fault, my parent's fault, my neighbor's fault, my preacher's fault. No, no, it's our responsibility to allow that love to grow inside of us.

Love Is Even GREATER When Others DON'T Take Care Of Your Stuff

Lastly, this. There's an even greater amount of love shown when you entrust something to somebody and *they don't take care of it* and you <u>still</u> love them.

Those people are called children. And I was a child, I was one of those people, too. I mean, if you're breathing, you either are or you were one of those people.

But imagine the parent who looks at the kid who just broke the window and says, "It'll be okay. We'll get it fixed." Even though the child may appreciate it and even though the child may value it, it takes a greater love on the part of the parent to overlook the sin and to love the sinner. To overlook the act, or in some cases, accident, and still love the person who was involved.

Back to the boat. Imagine that you own a boat with a friend. You're co-owners of a boat. They get to have fun with the boat. You get to have fun with the boat. It's an equal amount of dollars, equal time, equal repairs. When something breaks, it's split right down the middle. If it costs $400, that's $200 a piece. You use it the same. You pay for it the same. You always leave it full of gas. And you always leave it filled with oil. Everything's fine with the boat. It's rinsed, it's cleaned, it's waxed. Every time you leave it, it's ready for the next guy to use. And when you would show up and uncover the boat to get ready to use it, *you would expect that it be put away correctly.* That the rope be wound a certain way, that the anchor's ready to go, that it's not disappeared. You would expect that they hosed it off and if it's in the salt water, you rinse off the salt. If it's a fresh water boat, and it's been in the salt water, you have to rinse out the motor.

And you would expect that if you had done all those things, that when you show up to use the boat, *that it's been cared for by the other person just like you would care for it.*

Suppose that you show up to use it, you expect it to be ready, and you go to use it, and there's no gas. I don't know if you've ever filled a boat's gas tank but it isn't cheap. It's a lot of money. Let's say it's $100. And here you go, you show up to go fishing and there's $100 missing. Now all of a sudden you have to put $100 in the tank and when you leave you have to put another $100 in there because you're going to leave it for them in good shape. So now that one fishing trip costs you $200.

So now you expect to use everything on the boat. You expect all of the fishing rods to be where they're supposed to be. You expect the net to be where it's supposed to be. You expect everything to be ready to go. And you're going to put it away, ready for the other guy. It might mean extra time on your part. It might mean an extra sacrifice on your part. And oh well. I'm a partner in a boat. This is what I have to do. Because that's what partners do.

But what if you get there and the steering wheel is missing? You'd be like, "Well, what happened?" And you'd call your partner and they'd say, "Oh! Yeah, I took that home. I wanted to show it to a friend of mine. Sorry, I forgot to tell you."

Or what if you get there, and the engine is ruined. It seized up because there's no oil in it. "Oh, I forgot to tell you... now that you're offshore..." If you got there and it wasn't ready to work, you'd be upset. At best, you'd be disappointed. On the other side, you might be just a bit angry. Because it's not ready and that wasn't our deal. They've broken the boat!

The canopy, which I'm counting on to protect me from the sun, has holes in it! How'd that happen? "Well, I was fishing last time and I snagged it. I'm sorry. I didn't think it'd be a big deal."

Well, you know it's a big deal! And it's a big deal because we're partners. And we had an agreement that we'd keep this boat in a certain kind of shape that we agreed upon. And if it got broken, you'd be really sad.

However, to be able to forgive, and to move on from that... and to forgive doesn't mean to forget, by the way, it means to give up the right to get even... I'm not going to pay you back. But to be able to forgive and move on demonstrates a depth or a maturity of love.

That's God! That's Stewart, right there. Who has, more times than I could count, come to me and said, "Take care of my stuff," and I've not taken care of it well. And He still loves me. He still cares about me. Sometimes I don't put it away right. Sometimes I don't use it right. Sometimes I ignore Him. But He still loves me. And all Stewart's asking me to do is take care of the ship. But I'm too busy. I've got too many other things to do. I've got too many ideas. I've got a better plan.

And Stewart says it's not that hard. Take care of my stuff. Stay away from that over there.

"Eat whatever you want Adam and Eve. Don't touch that tree." That's stewardship from the beginning of the story. God says, "I said don't eat that tree. You can eat anything else. Don't touch that tree."

Isn't that what grace really is? Aren't stewardship and grace really connected?

I meet people who say, "I really love God. I long to be close to Him." Really? Because if we're really, really hungry for God, what will grow is our *faithfulness,* our passionate desire to protect His stuff. *Because His stuff is just there to be our stuff. We are joint-heirs. We are children of God. Our Father owns it and we get to use it. That's the benefit of being a child of the King.*

The resources that we have - time, talent, treasure, all of them - if we appreciate the fact and understand that *God is the one who gave them to us*, then we'll look after them. That's stewardship. That's grace. We call it amazing grace. Grace we didn't deserve. Grace we didn't earn. And yet He's willing to say, "You ruined my boat. Let's go for a ride." That's unbelievable.

Because we love Him, we protect His stuff. Because we love Him, we honor Him by doing what He's asks us to do, which is to stay away from *His* stuff. That's stewardship. Stewart's ship is amazing. Everything you could imagination.

Stewardship is not about dollars. It's about appreciation. And I'm asking you today, as we move forward On Purpose, understand that everything is God's. Nothing is ours. Psalm 24:1 - "The earth and everything in it is the Lord's."

That means I'm a steward. You're a steward. Of your house, your job, your kids, your food. You're a steward. Our job's just to take care of it. And present it back to God as a sacrifice. "I honor You God, by looking after Your stuff." That's stewardship.

How Do YOU Define Stewardship?

Our perspective on money is a tangible way, on a daily basis, for us to *understand the principles that God has established and to experience the provision only God can provide.*

Let's start with this:

When it comes to finances, there is always the worry that 'people don't want to hear about that' or that 'people are tapped out.' In some cases, people have a preconceived notion that the 'church' is only concerned about their money.

But here is the rub: we all need money in order to survive the daily grind. And in the end, everybody needs Jesus to survive the eternal grind. So you see, money and evangelism go together.

Why are we so afraid of these issues?

Maybe it's because they *require* us to get up and *DO something.* Let's be honest: sitting is easier. Even in our faith. It's much more comfortable to park somewhere they keep moving. Evangelism and tithing strike at the very heart of our choices, our plans and ideas. And these 'boundaries' have been set in place by US, "on purpose." They didn't get there by accident.

These words make us uncomfortable. Uneasy. We kind of feel yucky so we just avoid it. It's easier. It's tolerable.

Maybe they force us to look into the mirror and realize our duty and all that it requires. Maybe it raises the issue of personal responsibility in light of the free gift of grace. It's hard to admit; but we are not usually quick to offer 'strings free forgiveness' to those who offend us.

It's also hard to face the difficulties facing us where healthy, otherwise active Churchgoers settle for 'pew sitting' instead of really living for Christ. Living Life: On Purpose. We float down the river instead of swimming and exercising ourselves. We become 'CEO

Christians' (Christmas/Easter Only) and feel that 'we have done our part.' Sad part is that we become 'okay' with our minimal effort. That's not living. That's existing.

And then we feel 'guilt.' Could it be 'conviction' nudging us and nibbling at our hearts? When this happens we can either, face our shortcomings or run and hide. If we run, we still have to face ourselves, eventually. It's a strange thing, this 'self' we battle. We can't get away from ourselves, and we keep showing up all along the way. We sabotage our good intentions and work to destroy our progress.

Because of our 'consumer mentality' it's so easy to run to another church, hoping that it has no such requirement, so we can hide our inadequacies.

Oddly enough, it was through my church, my spiritual family, because of my faith in Christ, I received my gift of grace. But it seems that this 'membership' into the family of faith is more often set on the shelf. I use it from time to time, for my own benefit. So I can feel comfortable and safe. Weird: for the most part, God will let me keep it there. And all of a sudden that 'conviction' thing shows up again. It's in this moment that God is talking to me. Will I listen this time? Or will I pass it off as some emotion that I am trying to manage? Conviction is best managed by confession.

But, hey, that's the great thing about a 'no-strings-attached' perspective on grace. Nothing, and I do mean nothing, is required of me to be forgiven and nothing is required of me after this transformation.

But what good is a sports car that never moves? Or is only driven 35 miles per hour? *It is never given the chance to prove its worth! It's never allowed to live out its true purpose!*

Grace is provided and forgiveness is granted for sins that we confess to God. That is true. But as the book of James proclaims, what good is a faith (real faith) that is allowed to sit, collect dust and rust? What happens if we put feet on our faith and *actually DO something?*

I know this goes against the status quo and the American way of thinking. But *stewardship and evangelism can be exciting and rewarding.* They don't need to be scary. They can be fun!

The practice of stewardship is an act of love. And love is fun.

Mankind's greatest need is to be forgiven for our sins and put into a right relationship with God. All else considered, in the end, this is the only issue that really matters.

Stewardship is a response to God's love and grace. Because we have trusted Him with our greatest need and dilemma, He can be trusted with our daily needs. Our job is to take care of the things that belong to God. And according to Psalm 24 that's everything.

Read each of these verses: Proverbs 3:9-10; Romans 12:6

1. How do your personal perspectives (world-view) influence your beliefs and actions? How does it affect your outcome in serving and giving?

2. What does this Proverb have to say?

3. What does Paul have to say?

4. What does stewardship mean in these verses?

5. What does God want me to do with my Time, Talent and Treasures?

6. How can I have a better attitude about my money and resources?

7. How do you think God feels when we do not put to use what He gives us?

8. How have you forsaken your opportunities and responsibilities?

9. What has your church done with the resources and opportunities the Lord has given?

10. How has your church put its resources back into promoting the Kingdom? How can it do so better?

11. What does it mean to you that our God trusts you with His most valuable goods and people? What have you done? What will you do?

12. Do you really believe that real wealth in life is not in money, but rather in relationships and obedience? If not, why? If so, why?

13. How does it make you feel that when your talents are functioning as they are given to you, you become Christ's hands and feet in the world?

Remind yourself again:
        What is my purpose?

It's Not Up To Us

> "The earth is the LORD's, and everything in it, the world, and all who live in it." (Psalm 24:1)

Dictionary.com defines 'stewardship' as "the responsible overseeing and protection of something considered worth caring for and preserving."

Note the key words: responsible, overseeing, protection, considered.

For the Christian, as Scripture proclaims everything belongs to God. We are the managers of property, which belongs to God.

Since everything belongs to Christ, we need to have the attitude and view that *we don't own anything. Our stuff is His stuff. And His stuff is His stuff.*

Everything we have ever had, lost, misplaced, used, saved, invested, spent, accumulated or acquired belongs to Him *Including our spiritual gifts, our time, energy, health and our very lives.*

The 'responsibility' (see definition above) of the Christian is to *learn how to be true stewards of our Lord's resources that have been put in our care.* In fact, we are to manage them, to the *best* of our abilities *for His glory.* (1st Corinthians 4:2)/

It's possible that some Christians may have an issue with what I am trying to say here. This is one of those places where our thoughts and opinions really don't matter. What matters is what the Bible says.

The 'health and wealth' gospel has brought about the 'poor and destitute' gospel in some places. This idea that the "material world" is "not for the Christian" is not an new concept. It is an old-school religious thought called Gnosticism. This religious thought infiltrated the early New Testament church. In fact, much of Paul's writings were to confront the inaccuracies of this virus attacking the young, fledgling Church.

The truth is that the material world is God's too, and we are the stewards, the caretakers, of it. This includes anything that the eye can see, the mouth can taste, the ear can hear, the hands can touch or the feet can go.

This is our incredible *privilege.* God has placed in our care, all of His resources. All the parts of our lives: work, learning, spiritual gifts, relationships and our resources and interwoven in our physical and spiritual lives. And ultimately, these will all be used for God's glory or wasted. The result is largely due to our obedience or our laziness. And often our actions, either way, are 'on purpose.'

How Do I Look To God and not to Self

Look at it like this: Mankind is enjoying resources that God already owns. Some of us (the redeemed) are building a Church (the Body of Christ) among the creation. God has all the resources for this new building, all the equipment that we need, the plans for expansion and stability, and are plan for future growth and success.

There are opposing forces at work that do not want this building, or the concept of stewardship, to succeed. Storms come hinder the work. Complacency comes and that causes a stoppage or delay in growth. But, we can fight off this evil influence, with some spiritual fortitude (which takes hard work) and a personal will that is surrendered to God. Then the mission will succeed.

When we practice stewardship, it honors God with all of the relationships and resources in our life! Then we are able to show Him our gratitude for what He did for us. In addition, it helps us recognize His "Sovereignty" which is His control and ownership of all things. By doing this we honor Him with our worship as well as with our material goods and abilities.

Stewardship is a big deal. It is a priority! Why? *It is the most obvious, tangible way to show that we 'get it' and recognize that this isn't our 'stuff.'* We need to be satisfied with what we have, manage what we have and use it properly.

Stewardship is putting the gifts He gives into practice and not letting them waste away. This is an exciting thing! We discover our gifts and activate them with joy. If we have a gift that we don't use, that is wasteful. That's not good stewardship.

Stewardship is clearly demonstrated by being a faithful servant to Him. It is the understanding that who we are is based upon *who we are in Him and being thankful for grace.* And though we don't have to, we want to live in a way that God has instructed, (pleases Him) even though we don't have to. You see a life that please Him will most likely please us, too.

Stewardship is realizing that 'the church' is just a building. But "the Body of Christ" is truly 'the church.' If all we do is 'go to church' then we will just be existing in a building with other people and never accomplish His Purpose for our lives. But, if we live *as the Church,* then we can take the faith with us and live lives that bring Him great honor and glory.

Stewardship is not being foolish. In fact, it's just the opposite. Good stewardship is being wise to the ways of the world, so we do not fall prey to it.

Read each of these verses:

1 Corinthians 4:1-2; 6:19-20; Ephesians 5:15-16

1. What does Paul have to say?

2. What does stewardship mean in these verses?

3. How is Stewardship is a reflection of our spiritual condition?

4. Why should we never separate money and finances from our spiritual life?

5. How does Stewardship help you to recognize that you belong to Christ?

6. Do you see that being trustworthy, dependable, and honest is a matter of how you have or have not grown in Him?

7. The measuring stick that God uses to measure you is not against one another—what someone else has done, but rather what you are capable of.

So, how can this motivate you to take the opportunities He has given and make the most of them?

8. How have you misjudged yourself and the opportunities He has given?

9. Have you realized that when we negate our training, we will be unprepared and ill-equipped to do much of anything for His glory? How does this make you feel?

10. How does fear destroy your opportunity to be productive?

11. How can you do a better job at making Stewardship a priority?

12. How will your Stewardship honour God with all of your relationships and resources in your life?

Remind yourself again:

>What is my purpose?

Is Stewardship Really All That Important?

In the last two chapters we looked at what God calls responsible stewardship. We see where the Bible tells us that everything is His and that we are responsible for the care of His things. As Christians *who take the Bible seriously,* it's important that we realize and commit to the serious issue of being a wise steward.

Keep in mind that ultimately stewardship is an act of worship. It is based upon our gratitude in response to God's grace. Practicing stewardship helps *us* more than it helps God. *It forces us to acknowledge God's power and authority over our lives. In the end, it allows us to respond to His love by caring for what He brings into our lives.*

This is such a broad concept; everything in our lives is God's. Our relationships, time, spiritual gifts, material good, our money, our investments, our retirement accounts, our property, our homes, our children and grandchildren, our cabins and our mansions all belong to God. *Stewardship is our response to His most awesome creation, the grace He has shown us, as our way of saying thanks.*

We start by being thankful and this attitude leads to us caring for everything, yes, everything in our lives. So our gratitude for what *we do have* leads us to faithfully care for everything in this business that we call life. **Gratitude is also worship as our response to God's first loving us.**

In some evangelical circles stewardship is not seen as being all that important. Some people think that all that is required of Christians is to 'have a good heart' or to be sincere in their faith. The perspective is that our money and how we manage life is irrelevant.

But let me push back a little here: Is that true? Is God *only concerned with our heart? If that's the case, then what does that mean?* I confess that there have been phases of my Christian life that I have thought (believed…and lived by) this notion, too. What hit me between the eyes is that when I read the Bible (and you will see it there, too) it has a *totally different definition of stewardship that what I see in most Churches today.*

Read 1 Corinthians 16:1-4; 2 Corinthians 8:8-15

Check this out: Christ gave up His position and gave of Himself to save us. The widow gave what she had of herself through sacrifice (Mark 12; 41-44). The value of the 'gift' is directly the result of *what we are able to do*. At no time, **under no condition,** should we give what we do not have **and expect God to put it back in our account to cover the gift.** Besides the fact that this manipulates God, the book of Proverbs has a name for this kind of person. The book of Proverbs calls this person a fool.

Against popular opinion, good stewardship does not abuse the giver! The Bible does not command, teach, encourage or does Christ expect us to give *beyond our ability*. The 'giver' is not to abuse stewardship with false promises. Nor should they abuse it, with the best intentions, by giving what they don't have. No matter the motive stewardship does not demand what we can't give. Our faithfulness to give is *a response to grace, not a way to get more!*

Proper stewardship is supposed to be a regular, normal, and daily endeavour! It fits into every element of our lives. Our jobs, school and our hobbies. Stewardship *is the recognition of God's blessing for all things that we enjoy and participate in.*

Practicing good stewardship is the wise use of our resources, our physical material goods and abilities, as well as with our time. Wasting time, in the eyes of the Puritans, was a sin, and that notion did not originate with them, but with God's Word.

Proper stewardship is being not reckless, nor is it hiding from our duty by playing it safe. It is responsible and courageous.

Stewardship is recognizing that we, as Christians, as well as everything in creation, belong to God. In Florida, we are often asked about 'where we can find an alligator.' The saying here is, "If God made it there's an alligator in it." Well, if you can see it, God is in it!

Stewardship is directly proportionate to what we are able to give. The most meaningful things in life are not based upon their size but upon their value to the owner. The smaller gift is just as important as the larger gift! A diamond ring is much more valuable than a truckload of Styrofoam. It is very true that sometimes we cannot give as much as we would like to. Maybe this is due to economic realities, job loss, business not good, sickness, and so forth. And so, we give honestly and efficiently whatever we can.

Proper stewardship is an attitude; it's a perspective. It is the giving of ourselves and our resources with joy and gratitude for what we have been given. Stewardship is not something that results from a forced obligation or a bad attitude. Giving should always be cheerful! If it is not, then you are not really giving, are you?

Proper stewardship brings peace of mind. Why? It is the comfort of *knowing* that everything comes from God. Ultimately, He is the one who gives the understanding of how to live and please Him. It is a reality: We can trust in Him, and not in our materialistic goods.

Questions
Read Psalm 24:1; Acts 20:35; 2 Cor. 9:7; James 1:17

1. How can you make your life count for His glory?

2. Do you see stewardship as important? Why would some Christians think it is not?

3. How would is recognizing that we, as Christians, as well as everything in creation, belongs to God help with your attitude about Stewardship?

4. Do you believe that when we refuse to use what God gives us, we are being sinful? How so? Remember, this is not trivial, as it blocks His work from developing within us and through us to others!

5. What are the standards for stewardship we are to have?

6. Do you believe it is each Christian's responsibility to find, develop, and exercise the talents and gifts given to him or her? If so, what is in the way from this happening in you and in others?

7. What happens when we allow our fear to take us over?

8. How can you take comfort that God only gives us the opportunities to match the abilities He has given us? How would this help you eradicate your fear?

9. What do you need to do to allow Christ to let your confidence be who you are in Him, and not in how others respond to you? How would this help you learn and be confident in witnessing?

10. What do you believe God has given you? What have you done with it? Where do you invest what He gives you? How do you make it count for His glory? What now will you do about stewardship?

11. What can your church do to inspire and teach its people to have a better attitude about Stewardship?

12. How we serve and represent Him will also be a factor in our Judgment (not salvation but, rather, rewards). How does this motivate you to grow further? Or, does it scare you?

Remind yourself again:
        What is my purpose?

What Is the Right Amount To Give?

So what is the *right amount to give?* What's the right amount to give in a marriage? Is it *really* a 50-50 relationship? Or is it *really a 100-100 relationship?* If you spouse gave you 10% of their time and energy, would that be acceptable? Would that build the kind of intimacy that you want and need?

Do you remember chapter one? Our friend Stewart has a ship. He said you could use all the ship except 10%. And we call this *stewardship.* Not just tithing. We call that stewardship because *stewardship is about more than money.*

The 10% figure has been called a 'tithe' by the church for many years. I'm going to let you off the hook, so you don't have to worry about this 10% thing because some of you are like, "Dude, I make $2000 a month. There's no way that I can give 10%. There's no way I can give a tithe." Let's look at it some more.

I'm Going to Let You Off the Hook

We are called "New Testament Christians." This does not mean that the Old Testament is not important. It does not mean that the Old Testament is not true. And it doesn't mean that there aren't things in the Old Testament we can't learn from.

What it means is that in the Old Testament, the people of God did people things, activity, to prove they loved God, and they did things to appease God to make up for their sin. In the New Testament, Jesus comes as the Lamb, as the sacrifice, the substitute, the "propitiation," for our sin. And so we are no longer required to do certain things. Jesus has paid, ultimately, for our relationship with God. That's what a New Testament Christian is. It's that we live under grace instead of the law.

Not that the laws aren't right or true... the Ten Commandments are in the Old Testament. So we should learn from those things, but Jesus has paid for our sinfulness so that we cannot appease God except by accepting Christ. That's the only way to make God happy... to acknowledge that Jesus is the forgiver of my sin. Remember the A, B, C's of the cross: accept, believe, and confess. That's what a New Testament Christian is.

And because we're under grace... it's an amazing thing, but it's not to be taken for granted. "Mom, Dad, I poured that on the floor because I knew you'd forgive me." That's no different than, "God, I went and did that again... because I knew You would forgive me." That's an *abuse* of grace.

Okay, so here's where I'm going to let you off the hook. **The New Testament does not at all, ever, talk about tithing.** It doesn't talk about tithing. It does not say, "Give to God 10%." It does not say that. Then you say, "But then why does the church keep talking about it?" Because here's what the New Testament does teach: *gratitude*. And *graciousness*. And that's a lot bigger than 10%. "God I'm so thankful for what You did for me, that I'm going to be really, really gracious. I am going to be *generous*." That's what the New Testament teaches and that's far beyond 10%.

Remember Stewart? Stewardship is about appreciation. "God I get it. You did this for me so I'm going to do this for You. I love You this much. God I don't love you $2 worth. I love you $8 worth. I don't love you 2 hours a week's worth. I love you 20 hours a week's worth. I don't love you 3 chapters a week. I love you 40 chapters a week." It's about appreciation.

"God, I get it! You did something for me so I'm going to show you how much I appreciate it and I'm going to do something for You. You gave me this great big boat. You let me drive it. You gave me everything on it. All you asked is that I stay out of that one room that belongs to You." So how in the world does this
10% belong to God if the New Testament doesn't talk about it?

Because the whole boat is His. That's why. It's *100%* His. He's just willing to let you use it. And all He said was that I just don't get to use that part. It's 10%. And it's not just your finances. It's your time. It's your talent. It's your effort. That's what this is about.

Stewardship is about you and I taking care of the things God has given to us. Some of you have incredible talents and have never, and I will use the word "never", used them for the Kingdom. Some of you are great teachers, some of you have great leadership skills, some of you are great organizers, some of you are great servers... some of you are great at all these different gifts that God gives! Read about them in the New Testament. He didn't give them to you. The Bible says He gave them for the common good. And yet we've kept our gift, and buried it in the back yard, because we don't want anyone to touch it. you might use it up. Don't bother me. Don't ask me to get involved. Leave me alone! I don't want to work with the children. I don't want to work with the youth. I don't want to work with women. I don't want to work with men.

And so what happens is Pastor Tom hits a wall. There's only one doorknob on that door and it's on your side: you have the knob! I don't. I can't get there. And so the church crawls when we could fly.

How can we fly? Because the Bible teaches, there are enough gifts here to be the Church God wants us to be. Now aren't you tired of being the church we've decided to be? Don't you want to be the Church He wants us to be?

Stewardship is about appreciation! So I sing from the bottom of my heart, and I sing loud. Why? Because I don't care of it's good! Because I love God.

Pastor Tom, people don't sing anywhere but church. Sure they do! People sing all over the place. When you're walking through the grocery store, and you're in a good mood, you're singing along with the radio. You don't care if you can't sing. Why? Because it does something in your spirit and you just want to sing because you're happy. You appreciate it.

Stewardship is something that you demonstrate. I've been married for thirty years. And if after awhile I don't tell my wife, "I love you," don't you think she's going say, "What?"

You have to say it! "Oh but I told God once when I was fourteen." I get that. You were at youth camp. We all did that. You've got to say 'I Love You' everyday! The people that you live with... if you don't tell them every day, "I love you," they're going to assume at some point, "You don't love me." Even if they can't talk back!

I've got a little rugrat at my house . He can't talk to me. But I tell him every day, "Lucas, Doc loves you." Why? Because I want him to know it! I want to remind him. We forget. Especially when you get old. We forget.

I remember one time when my daughter, Tori, was little, she used to hug my Dad and tell him, "Crapaw, I love you." And he said, "I know, but don't ever stop telling me." Don't you think he knows after 21 years? Well, yeah, but he still wants to hear it. And when you get on the phone with your kids, especially an adult child that's sort of responsible, and you're on the phone with them helping them do something, don't you want to hear as they get off the phone, "Love you Mom and Dad." Isn't that what you want to hear? Or do you want to hear, "Hey thanks for the $300. *click*." At least they said thanks. Gratitude is something that you show.

And stewardship is something that's directly related to our spiritual maturity. Your self-sacrifice, my self-sacrifice, is directly related to my spiritual maturity. In other words, I should be giving more time, effort, money, dollars, whatever this year than I gave last year. And the year before. And the year before. Everything that I'm entrusted with... I should be doing more than what I have previously. Why? Because I love God.

We can argue with God all we want. But it does not matter what we think. It matters what the Bible says. So if we're going to be New Testament Christians, then let's live what the New Testament says. What Jesus says. Not just about giving. But about sacrifice, because really, ultimately, that's what stewardship is all about. Because it doesn't matter what I think, it doesn't matter what you think. It matters what the Bible says.

This is it records Jesus as saying, in your Bible.

"There was a certain rich young ruler, who asked Him [Jesus] saying, 'Hey Good Teacher... (notice what he says) what shall I do to inherit eternal life?'..." In other words, "In case I haven't got it yet, what do I need to do?"

"Jesus said to him, 'Why are you calling me good? There's only one person that's good and that's God. Well, young man, you know the commandments, don't you? Don't commit adultery, don't murder, don't steal, don't bear false witness, and you should honor your father and mother.'" And the guy's thinking, "I'm in like Flynn!" All I have to do is keep these things the rest of my life because I've kept these things from my youth. I kept the Law.

And then Jesus says to him, "Just one thing you lack." This would surely indicated that he's not in the kingdom yet. "You lack," Jesus said.

And Christ says, "Sell all that you have and distribute it to the poor." Which means, if he has that much, everyone's poor compared to him. "And then you'll have treasure in heaven. And follow me."

So I've got to sell my stuff, give it away, and *submit to following Jesus to inherit the kingdom of heaven.* So we have to be willing to let God be God of our resources... and God of our lives to inherit the Kingdom.

You can keep all the rules you want. If you don't do those two things, you don't inherit the Kingdom. "And when he went away, he was very sad." Why? He didn't want to give up either one. He didn't want to give up his stuff. But he didn't want to give up his will, either. He could have followed and kept all his stuff. But he didn't do that. He went away sad, instead. That's what Jesus said.

So what's the New Testament standard for giving? What's the right amount?

Zacchaeus... remember that story? Zacchaeus is up in the tree, Jesus sees him, and calls him down. He's a tax collector. His job is to go around and tax people.

At times, he would find people and say, "I'm going to make you pay more." So he would steal and keep the difference. Jesus confronts him. Then Zacchaeus says, "I'll give half of what I own to the poor. And the people that I stole from, I'll give them their money back times four."

So out of the remaining half, if he stole from people, he paid them back four times as much. So he gave back more than half. So the New Testament so far as two stories. One is half. The other is all.

Let's just say you make $30,000 a year. Can you imagine? That every time you get a paycheck, you're just going to sign the whole thing over. That's "all." Can't imagine that, right? Why? Because you have bills to pay. God understands that. So what is he saying? "I'm not asking for all of it. What I'm asking for is the right amount." And the "right" amount, believe it or not, is different. The "amount".

In the Old Testament, the tithe was something that the Hebrew people had to do. It was required. It was not optional. It was not a tax. It was a *minimum,* not a *maximum.*

I've run into people who say, "Well, I'm not giving more to the church. I've already given my tithe." I want you to picture what that's saying. You're saying that tithe is a maximum. The Bible teaches that the tithe was a minimum. They had to give 10% to fund the government, the chief priests and so on... then they had to give 10% for the priests of the synagogue... then they had to give another 10% to the poor. And what they would do is farm their fields in a square, they would harvest in a circle, and then let the poor have the outside edge. They considered that their tithe. And then, if there was a special tax, they had to give even more. So they had to give a minimum of 30%. That's a lot of tithes. Right?

So the people gave and they gave and they gave and the 'tithe' was not looked at as a maximum.

But the tithe is *not permission* to do less. *It was an opportunity to do more.* But it was a way to systematically judge how you were doing. That's the way it is in the church. We look at it and say how am I doing compared to last year? Remember maturity means that I should be growing. So I should be doing better than I did last year. That's what stewardship is all about. So our giving shows what's going on in our heart. And it's everything.

"Pastor Tom, I was looking at our church's budget, and it seems right here that we're really heavy in salaries." Do you know why? Because we have to pay people to do the work of ministry. Do you know why? Because there aren't volunteers who will do it for free. The Pastor's responsibility is not *to do the work* of ministry, alone. The Pastor's job, according to the Bible, is to *administer the ministers.* The Pastor is to guide and oversee and direct the Church family, while you do the work of the ministry. That's the Bible perspective.

So the reason we have associate staff, people that we pay nickels and dimes here and there, is because we need to make sure they're going to keep doing it . It builds a relationship with us. Makes them an official part of what we're doing. But it's because we don't have anyone who stepped up along the way who said, "I want to do it for free." That's really why. *The Bible teaches us that the spiritual nature can over come the human nature.* It's the Biblical perspective. God has been so good to us, we want to show Him gratitude. It's a maturity issue.

So What Is the Right Amount?

If I were to come to you and say, "In my hand, I have the magic potion. This will make it right between you and God for all time. All you have to do is write me a check. That's all you've got to do. You can spend an eternity in heaven." You would pay every dime that ever came your way, that you ever made, so that you could do this.

If you were sick and this was the cure, if this was for your kids... those of us that have kids, when they're sick... if this could cure them, you'd do whatever it takes. That's what grace is. But the weird part about grace is you don't have to pay for it. All you have to do is accept it. It's already been paid for. Salvation wasn't free. Grace wasn't free. It cost Jesus His life. It cost God His son. However, all you have to do is say, "I want that." But how much would you give? How much money would you really, really give?

Shared Risk, Shared Return. It's like insurance. Why doesn't that work in the church? It does work in the church. Because God exponentially multiplies His money. I don't know how it happens. It just happens. Many of us have seen it happen.

The sacrifice you make today is because you love your family or to plan for your future, right? That's why you want to put this money aside. You say "no" to yourself as an investment for the future. You get to live through your heirs because you helped fund whatever it is they're going to go do.

You won't hear Pastors do this very often, but here goes: I want to give you permission to be selfish. I want you to stop hoarding your money and give it away while you're alive so that you can see the smile on someone else's face. I want you to be so selfish, you say, "That's what I'm living for. I'm living to see people come to Christ. I'm living to see lives changed. I'm living to see marriages put back together." Be selfish. Invest your time. Invest your money into seeing people's lives changed. That's what this is about. And this ship of stewardship is a love condition. If you love Him, it's no big deal.

So what's the right amount? What does the New Testament say? Imagine you're part of a team. I'll pick a team, only because I know their names. Let's say you're part of the University of Alabama football team. You're part of a team. It doesn't matter what position you play. It doesn't matter if you play. If you wear the jersey and travel, you're with the team. And if the team wins something, you get a copy of it. If they win a National Championship or a Superbowl, you get a ring. Even if your'e the front office guy for whatever team, you get all the spoils for the hard work of other people.

But when you're part of a team, this is what they ask for. *You get an equal reward, but you make an equal sacrifice.* **Whatever you do, do it your best.** It really doesn't matter if you're the holder, doesn't matter if you're the water boy. Do it the best you can do it and I'll do my job the best I can do it and when we get to the end, we'll all have an equal reward. That's what being a team is about.

It's not equal activity. It's equal *effort*. Effort is the key word here. The Olympics are different. They are different because I can go and give my best and we're not all going to get the same award. It is entirely possible I may be the worst 100m guy at *the Olympics,* but I made it to the Olympics because I'm the fastest guy in my country.

So when we get together at the beginning of the season, the goal is to win the championship. Everything else is failure. We want to win the championship. It doesn't matter what the score is in the middle of the game. At the end, we want to be holding the championship.

Nick Saban, coach of Alabama, says no matter what happens, his phrase is "You do your part." Doesn't matter what the score is. You do your part. And if your job is to knock big people down, then knock big people down. Let the guy who catches the ball worry about catching the ball. You just knock people down. Do your part. Because the goal is to win the championship. *So you give your best because that's what your team deserves.* The team deserves that when you're running, and you go to knock someone down, because that's your job, you don't watch the guy run by you. You try to knock him down.

What about times I may fail to get my part accomplished?

If we all lived on a farm and your job is to collect eggs, we understand that one day you get up and you have the flu. I'll go collect your eggs.

But we *don't understand* if you come to the breakfast table and say, "I really just didn't feel like collecting eggs today." We don't understand *lazy. And lazy ain't sexy*. You see, we're hungry and the team deserves eggs. And you're job is to go get eggs. So teams are made of equal sacrifice, equal reward.

The difference is you're not a part of a team. You're a part of a *family*. This is family. We're in this together. We like you. Hopefully you like us. The fact is that you're invested here and we've invested in you. But the *family* needs you to do your part. Equal reward, equal sacrifice. Because that's what families do.

And that's what stewardship is. Equal effort. *Not an equal "amount"*.

Equal effort. I'm going to do my best. Not what's comfortable. My best.

And the Church family is trusting every other person in the family to do their best. Because that's what families do. All God is asking is that you do your best. Give your best.

Don't write a check and say, "Oh yeah, that's my best." That's Ananias and Sapphira. Read about it in Acts 5.

Paraphrased, it goes like this: "Oh yeah... um, we got this money.... didn't you sell some land? Oh no! We didn't sell any land. Yes you did. No! We didn't sell any land. We know you sold some land!"

And what happened? They died. Why? They lied. They lied to the family of faith and they lied to God. *They tried to hold back what they had.* They tried to give some money and say, "We're not kidding, this is our best." And it wasn't.

Give the family what's best. **The right amount is your best.** Time, talent, investment, dollars, give your best. Because that's what stewardship is. And don't hold back. Don't wait. What are you waiting for?

Along the way, every now and then, I run into families where the story always has the same line in it, and it never has a happy ending.

It goes like this: "I wish I would have..." Then fill in the blank.

"We got up like we always do and got into a fight about orange juice. And I wish I..."

"I don't know what happened. My kids went off to college and I wish I would have..."

The story always starts the same. "I wish I would have..."

Stop wishing. And start Living Life, On Purpose. Invest in the Kingdom with your time, talents, and treasures.

That's true stewardship.

What's Right or What's Left?

For this section, you will need to grab a Bible and turn to 2nd Corinthians Chapters 8 and 9.

What you will notice here is that God gives great weight and value to *what is in our hearts, and that a good heart has a responsible character element to it.* This is what being a good steward is all about. In the Hebrew language 'stewardship' means "house law and rule." It would mean that whoever is hired to oversee the affairs for the owner. It might include the property, resources, money and all of the provisions are *all under the steward's control and responsibility.* **All of our resources belong to God and are entrusted into our hands for safe keeping.** That's a big responsibility.

Keep in mind that every angle, every detail of 'management' is found in the word and theme of stewardship. Everything that we do in our daily lives is part of stewardship, too!

Is God concerned with your heart? Yes! He is! And being a good steward will show you that you have a good heart!

It is not possible for a good, responsible steward to be wasteful. In Bible times, wasteful stewards were killed. Can you imagine if we still did this today? The way we waste food, electricity, hot water, energy and time? There would be a lot of dead people around!

Good thing for us we have access to, and hopefully, experienced God's grace. This means we are not subject to His wrath because of Christ's sacrifice. His 'atonement' for us gives us another 'chance' *but that does not mean we should be careless or wasteful.*

It also means that all we need to do is 'think we are good.' *Our perspective* is not God's perspective. What *He thinks* is what truly matters. Just because we think we are good at school, or the best on the team or the most valuable at work does not change the facts. In stewardship there is no time to slack off or become complacent. *We have to think clearly and carefully about the most effective, efficient way to invest and manage all the gifts and resources He has entrusted to us!* This is all in response to the gift He has given to us of His grace, love, mercy and care.

Tough question:
Are You Giving God What's Right or What's Left?

The Biblical perspective is that we are poor stewards when we waste anything that God has given to us. This wastes our lives and plenty or opportunities, too! You see stewardship is more than just a 'heart' issue! Sure, a good heart is important. But a 'good heart' leads to 'good behaviors.' But if we are not careful and let our guard down, even for a moment, we can become irresponsible. And when that happens, our hearts can be affected, too

Everybody needs less stress in their lives. I would guess you would love to eliminate just a little bit of the worry from your list of daily concerns and activities. This little tip can take one item off your prayer list.

Stewardship is the elimination of worry, and replacing it with trusting in Christ.

Stewardship helps take our eyes off of self and look out for His interest as well as the concerns of others.

Stewardship is the confidence that God is concerned with us individually, intimately and personally. He cares about what we go through, have to face and how we manage what He entrusts to us.

With all the talk about a 'positive mental attitude' it seems to me that stewardship really is the 'attitude of gratitude' in being appreciative and thankful for all things, even things we do not feel gratitude or see it.

Proper stewardship analyses, not ad nausea, and sees every purchase as an investment, from food and gas, to houses and cars. It considers the long term value and worth of each expenditure.

Proper stewardship is centred on God, His objectives and His activity. It is not focused on the material things, in and of themselves. We should always see the 'stuff' with the perspective that we are God's caretaker of it. We must guard against the greed or covetous nature that 'things' can create.

Proper stewardship is about being in community. No man is an island and no giver is either. We work together, with other believers, complementing each other's gifts and giftedness, with what we can offer. When we use these gifts correctly, we can do great things. This is how we use the gifts that He has given to us to benefit those in our local church and those around us.

Questions

Read Matthew 6: 25-34:

1. How are worry and the ability to give connected?

2. What about our time? Do you always live in a rush? If so, does that please God? Does it leave time for important things, such as relationships and ministry?

3. What is Righteousness? What about the Body and Kingdom of God?

4. Read Ephesians 5:15-21

5. Write a list of the priorities in your life. Then, with the above verses in mind, ask yourself," How do my priorities line up with God's?"

6. What can you do to line your up your priorities to be more like God's?

7. How can you do this more?

8. How *are* you using your gifts for the Body and the glory of Christ?

9. How *can* you use them for the Body and for Christ's glory?

10. Why does our Lord so often cite the use of money as an illustration?

11. How does the abuse of money to oppress the poor dishonour our Lord? Do you believe that stewardship is a matter of the heart? Take a look at your check book; it will show where your loyalties, commitments, and interests abound!

12. How would you define ethics? How does this effect Stewardship?

13. How does what we chase become temporary and rotten? Have you considered that the things we think are important usually are not, such as trust in wealth, accomplishments, education, self, or ? Why would we place our trust in this stuff and not in the One who loves us?

14. If you are not responsible, chances are, no, you do not have a good heart. Do you agree? Why or why not? What are you going to do about this question?

Remind yourself again:
        What is my purpose?

Giving Until It Hurts

My high school Chemistry teacher would begin *every class session* with the same statement: "Man is a creature of habit. And Man is basically lazy." Unfortunately, there is probably a shred of truth in there.

I've run into people all over the place who say, "The church needs money? But I've already given my tithe." A tithe isn't a maximum. A tithe is a standard minimum that we should look at and think, "Oh I gave 10%." What seems to happen to many of us is that when we get our giving statement at our church, and we open it up and think, "Oh, I thought I did better than that." I understand.

I know it's hard to sit down and write out a check. I know it's hard to support your church with the first payment every month. I know it's hard to do it online. *But mankind is a creature of habit.* The point is, if you get into the habit of doing something, pretty soon it becomes something that you do.

Creatures of Habit

Have you ever noticed that you put your shoes on in the same order every day? Have you ever noticed, right foot goes in first, or left foot goes in first? Have you ever noticed doing it wrong one day and saying, "Wait! Something's wrong."

Have you ever noticed you go to work the same path every day. Why is that? You may say, "It's the shortest route." Well, there are other paths. You could go another way. Try it and see what happens. You'll be so out of sorts. You won't know what to do. Why? Because we're creatures of habit.

How many of you mix your food up on your plate? How many of you, the food is not even allowed to touch? And if somebody mixed it up, you would say, "No! No, no, I can't eat that." Because you have developed a habit of how you do it.

Mankind is a creature of habit. We do the same thing, the same way, over and over and over again. In Proverbs, it says, "Just like a dog returns to its vomit, a fool will repeat his folly." We have habits and we do the same thing even though it makes no sense. Mankind really is a creature of habit.

We Love Comfort

And we love comfort. We don't like being just a little bit out of sorts. How many of you remember wooden pews in church? How man you don't even know what a pew is? A pew is a long wooden bench. It has a wooden back but it's a long bench. So you didn't have chairs, just a long bench. And in churches, way back when, until about the 70's, churches had pews. These immovable pieces meant that you couldn't use this room for anything else. Because the pews would be right where we are. Churches, in order to be able to use the room for more things, went to chairs.

When I was a kid, I didn't have children's church. I had to sit in church and behave. And listen. And when I went home, my parents asked me about the sermon because I was expected to listen.

A friend of mine did his masters thesis on the effects of children's church compared to the attendance of college kids in traditional church. What he found was in the late 70's children's church became a big thing. It became McDonald's play land in church. Systematically, 13 or 14 years later, attendance of college students in church dropped.

Oh you say, "In children's church, we're planting seeds in the minds of these children." I get that concept, for sure. But what it indicates is that everything was catered to them. Children's ministry, youth group, all this was catered to the child, then when they go to college, they have to go to big church, and they don't know how to respond or interact. They don't know how to participate. Because this isn't about them anymore. And there was a corresponding drop in attendance to children's church attendance.

You say it doesn't happen. Yeah, it does. Many of us in church today disappeared from church from the ages of 18-25 or 30, until we got married and had kids, then we come back to church because we know the stability that it brings.

We just don't like being uncomfortable. "It's too hard for me to keep giving money. I'm uncomfortable, I don't want to do it. I don't want to go to the dentist. I don't want to have my teeth cleaned or pulled. I don't want to take my car in and get it serviced. I don't want to be uncomfortable." And because we're creatures of habit, we tend to avoid anything and everything that we don't care for. We don't really want to deal with what is the problem.

And the truth is the same with our finances. "My finances are on fire, my life is on fire, I can't pay my bills, and if I ignore it long enough, it will go away." No, if you ignore it long enough, you will go away. People will find you. They're not going to give up until they get what they're after. And to ignore your woes and stick your head in the sand, is not going to make them go away.

Besides that, if what you've always done got you there, and you keep doing what you've always done, you're going to stay there. I have learned the hard way, you have to take finances by the horns, and get control of it. And you have to deny yourself and then move on. You cannot sit and wait for everyone else to solve your problem because it won't happen. Creatures of habit, sure, but we can't be afraid to be uncomfortable. We have to find a way to make ourselves uncomfortable.

Here's what happens. The church creates opportunities for you to be *"spiritually irritated."* That's the best I can describe it. We want you to think, "Oh, I don't like this!" We want you to do that! Why? Because then you will walk away from the ministry opportunity saying, "Oh, that was really great." That's what will happen!

Those of you who been to a third world country, where you couldn't drink the water, when you got back you said, "I can't wait to go again." Because you get there, and you hug and kiss those kids and you can't wait to go back. It really doesn't matter how uncomfortable you were abothe water. Water is no big deal!

So we create missions opportunities so you and your family can serve here in town. We want you to be just a bit uncomfortable. *Because that's when spiritual growth happens.* Because we get into habits with our spirituality, too. And some of them are bad habits.

Face it, if you keep doing what you have always done, you're going to stay exactly where you are spiritually. You're not going to grow. So the Church provides opportunities for you to grow. And in order for you to do that, you have to get out of your box, just a lot.

And there's nothing like growth happening in moments when we're just uncomfortable. So that's why we create those opportunities.

And that's what stewardship is. I've got a life. I can invest my life. I can invest my time, I can invest my energy, I can invest my money. I can do one. I can do two. Or I can do all three. The level of growth is up to you.

When we get into the habit of "doing" we will usually continue "doing" because you are a creature of habit. And stewardship ultimately is a direct reflection of spiritual maturity.

Here's the rub: If you're saying you're growing, then you're telling me you're experiencing the spiritual growth that comes from good stewardship. There's no other way to say, "I'm growing," if you're not being a good steward. It just can't happen. Biblically, it doesn't work that way.

And the truth is we want to argue with God about all of this. "But God, I don't like being uncomfortable. I can't take care of these people." And I've said that myself. "I don't want to do that. I don't like that. I'd really prefer not to do that."

And God's whole point is, "So? Who cares what you want." What I think or what I feel doesn't matter. What matters is what the Bible says.

Last Sunday, when we finished service, a service about giving the right amount, I'm getting ready to go home and a guy walked in here, I've never met before, and said, "I need gas. I've got to get to work tomorrow." I said, "Oh, okay" I've heard this story a trillion times. I asked him where he works. He told me. I asked him what kind of car he drives. He tells me. I asked him where he needed to drive to get to work. And he tells me. I asked how much money he needed. He said, "I don't need a lot. Maybe $10. Just to get some gas. And you can follow me to the gas station, and you can pay for it, and I'll be on my way."

I'm not going to lie to you. I didn't have time for this. Are you kidding me? Like I want to stop at the gas station and buy you gas? I don't know you. I was sure it was a scam.

As I'm getting my stuff together and I see that this guy is waiting for me. And I thought, "You know what. I just told these people you've got to do what's right."

And so I thought about it. And I drove down to the gas station. I thought I'd get some gas, too. I pulled up and put gas in his car. $20 in his car. $20 in my car.

And I thought, "You know what. I don't know who that guy is. I don't know who sent him here. Why'd he come that day?" But what would have happened if I'd said, "God bless! Be warm, well fed, I'll pray for you." $20 isn't *really* a sacrifice.

And I walked away from it thinking, "I don't like this God. I feel like I just got scammed."

And God's whole point was, "So? So what? $20 to do something that was kind?"

You see I'm one of these foolish people that says what I think, which often gets me in trouble. But, truthfully, I am not a terribly compassionate person. Sure, I care about people and all that but every fiber in my body was saying "See ya!"

I don't why that this time it was different, because there have been plenty of times that I've said "see ya".

But this time... doesn't matter what we think. It matters that we're righteous and we do right things. Because that's what the Bible teaches us.

Giving until it hurts... Galatians 2:20 says, "I [Paul] have been *crucified*...." [That sounds bad already]. "I have been *crucified* with Christ."

I want you to pay attention to this part. "It's no longer me who lives. But it's Christ who lives in me. And the life that I now live in this flesh, I live by faith in the Son of God who loved me and gave Himself for me."
This isn't my life. I didn't buy the guy gas. I was just the vehicle that God used to put $20 in the machine so he could have gas. My life belongs to God. My doings belong to God. Everything that I do is supposed to represent God. And I don't think God would have said, "Too bad."

This life that I now live in the flesh, I live by faith in the Son of God who loved me and gave Himself for me. What does that mean? I am crucified. That's giving until it hurts. Crucified. Not $20. Not $200. *Crucified is when it hurts, and not until.*

This life I live, I live by faith in the Son of God.

We don't want to be uncomfortable. Ask any dentist. It's the perfect example. We'll let that tooth fester. We'll let it get as big as a chipmunk before we go to the dentist. And what do they always say? "If you would have come here when this first started, I could have taken care of this."

Every time you go to get your car fixed, you here a pinging sound. And you think, "That'll go away." Sure enough, we take it in and what do they say? "If you'd brought it, then this wouldn't have gone bad, and that wouldn't have gone and this wouldn't have gone bad."

Mankind is *very predictable*. But that doesn't make it okay that we're creatures of habit. *We need new habits*. Generosity would be one. Kindness would be one. Compassion. I understand that we've got to protect ourselves, do what we can to look after our stuff, our people. I get that. But there's a side of it where we're supposed to care about other people too.

[Missing portion due to video malfunction.]

What He does promise is that He'll meet our needs. "The Lord's my Shepherd, I shall not want." In the Living Bible, "I've learned to be contentment with all that I have."

"You know... I need a new TV." Need? "Well, yeah, I need a 55" TV." Well, what's wrong with the 50" TV? "Oh the picture now is much better."

Need? No, you need food, water, shelter, clothing... ESPN. Need and want are two different things. Because I promise you, we don't have to go very far to find people who have no TV. None. We don't even have to leave Orange County to find people who don't have a television.

"I need new tennis shoes." How much are those tennis shoes? "$145" Seriously? You ever heard of Payless? Ross?

I remember, back when I was a kid, "I need some jeans. $80 Gloria Vanderbilt jeans." The girls had to have them. Seriously? Sears Rough Rider jeans were real jeans. Mom would iron on patches in the knees. They were so stiff you couldn't even walk in them. $5 each. Remember those? They were like steel. Couldn't wear those things out.

Need. "I need..." Careful when you say the word "need." Because "need" means, "I'm not satisfied with what I have." "I need a new phone." You have a phone. "Yeah but the new ones do so much more stuff." Yeah they play more games. That's it. It's a phone. You used to hang phones on the wall. You had to hang out in the garage to talk on the phone with your girlfriend. That was only if you had the really long cord.

This is a hard battle for us because we always want the newest, latest, and greatest. I get that. That's why they came out with the phrase "2.0". It's all about the dollar at some point. Somebody somewhere is making money. I get that.

However, the battle for us is to be content with the stuff that we have. God doesn't want us to go without. But He doesn't want us to abuse this idea that I can go get more and more and more, and build up this arsenal of stuff that you're not taking with you.

We buried my mother-in-law yesterday. I saw her. She had on cosmetic jewelry, a cosmetic jewelry necklace, and she was in a box with a pair of pants and a blouse and a shirt and that's it. And you know what? She didn't even get to take that with her. Do you know why? *She didn't need it. She didn't need that stuff.*

God cannot be manipulated by your giving either. "I want God to bless me so I'm going to find the name of a church online and I'm going to send them $25 so God will keep blessing me." Thanks for the $25. *God is not obligated to bless you because you gave him money.* **He's obligated to bless you because He loves you.** Not because you did something to try to get Him to do something. "I'm going to give Him $25 because the Bible says He's going to give it to me 10 times back." No, it doesn't say that. I can make it say that. But it does not say that.

You cannot go to the First National Bank of God and somehow make a deposit, then make a withdrawal that is ten times the amount. God does not promise that. And anyone, anywhere who ever tells you anything other than that is lying to you.

You should never, never give to God in order to get from God. "Oh, my Aunt needs healing so I'm going to make a $1000 donation to my church because God will be impressed with that and somehow that'll get more favor from God." These are terms you hear all over the place. That's not how this works. God is going to intervene and heal your Aunt, if that's what His will is because God loves your Aunt and because God wants to do what's good. That's why. You cannot manipulate God. "I'm going to get God on the line! I'm going to throw the bait out there, God took it, wow!, I'm going to reel God in now, ten times the amount..."

No. It doesn't work like that. *But you should always give to God because you appreciate what He did for you and because you love Him.* That's why you give. It's not for any other reason.

And so when we give what we have been known to call "tithes and offerings", *it's always a sacrificial gift.* It's always because you love God. And you love Him a lot! So you give a lot.

And you give your time and talent as well as your treasure because you love God a lot. And stewardship is a love condition. And because I love Him, I've got to give Him a bunch of everything I've got because it's His anyway. You're just acknowledging that it's His. It's a heart condition.

When you go to the doctor, they look at you, they run some test, they tell you, "Hey you've got a heart problem." And you say, "Oh, no I don't." They say, "No really you do." "No I don't. I'm fine. I'll be fine." And the doctor will do everything they can to try to get you to do something about your heart and I'm trying to tell you, you don't have to go to the doctor.

Look at your stewardship.

What are you doing with your life? What are you doing with your time? What do you do with your thoughts? What do you do with your study time? What do you do with your money? What do you do with your free time? Do we sit around and fill our minds with what everyone else is thinking or do we go to God and say to Him, "I want to know what You think." That's stewardship.

We have to do our best. That means we always have to be prepared. When you're getting ready to move, you start weeks ahead of time, boxing, taping, getting everything labeled. Ready to go. Big day comes and all of a sudden, the saying goes, "Organization is the keynote to success."

The same thing can be said of our stewardship. *You've got to be prepared.*

"What am I going to do if all of a sudden I got this money? What would I do if $1000 fell out of the sky?" Because sometimes, blessings surprise us.

Sometimes, when you least expect it, something happens, you get a raise, you get promoted, you get a commission check, or a tax return, whatever... and it's just a big surprise! You've got to be prepared. What am I going to do with that? How am I going to look at that? And the typical, American way of looking at that is, "Oh! I got $178. Let's go shopping! I wasn't counting on that."

However, to a person of faith, realizing that the $178 belongs to God, asks, "how would God want me to use that $178? Maybe God would want me to do something else!" And so you get yourself prepared!

I'm going to expect God to show up, sometime. Might be tomorrow. Might be today. Might be in December. But when He shows up, this is what I'm going to do with this money. I'm going to take that $178 that I wasn't planning on anyway, which belongs to Him, and I'm going to give it because somebody else is going to hear about Jesus."

"Now God, if I don't get that $178, I can't give it."

*Our giving, our tithing, if you will, our regular giving is to be **our best**. Those gifts are from money that we are pretty sure we can count on.* We know it's coming in.

What about the "surprise" money? I'm asking you to take that surprise money and time and say, "I'm going to do this with it. God I promise You, that when this comes in, this is how I'm going to give it. I promise You."

So if God gives it, you promise to give it. If God doesn't give it, you can't give it.
It's up to God to provide the money. If there's no money, there's no ministry. You don't have to worry about it. God does His thing. That's His part of the process and it's up to you and I to be good stewards of the money He provides.

Remember, all you have to do is your best.

I would guess that some of you are saying, "Tom, I'm already doing my best. I am *really* already doing my best." *Really?*

I don't know if you know it or not, but around the world, Christians are still killed every day. And I don't mean sometimes. I mean every day, someone; somewhere is being killed because of the name of Christ. Men and women are being imprisoned because they are ministers or missionaries. Many, many missionaries, to this day, have to function under cover because they're scared that if somebody finds out, they'll be put to death. But they're there to be missionaries for Christ and if they're caught, they can die.

Back in the 70's, in the Eastern world, in parts of China, Bibles were being smuggled in and missionaries were trying to get in there. There was a situation where my home church supported a Chinese mission. A local was recruited and trained as a Christian pastor. I heard stories about how the police would come down the street and knock on the door and out of fear, the people would go and hide. They would go to the basement, hide in closets, under beds, wherever they could because they knew if they were captured, they would be killed.

And this national was caught; he was captured by the authorities. And he was put in prison.

For his punishment, they tied him, bound him, and hung him upside down in his cell. And they would swing him back and forth.

That didn't seem to be enough of a punishment. So they took a very large container and put dog feces in it. Every time he swung over the dog feces, his face would be dragged through the feces.

Do you know what he's saying while this is happening?

He sang, because he was content. He was in prison. He was facing death. He was hanging upside down, swinging through feces. And he sang.

"What a friend we have in Jesus. All our sins and griefs to bear."

And as if that wasn't bad enough, eventually they set the container on fire and they swung him back and forth over the dog feces set on fire.

"All because we do not carry, everything to God in prayer."

And that man died. Singing.

Make this your statement of stewardship: "I am crucified with Christ. And the life I live, I don't live this life for me anymore. It's the life I live in You. Because You loved me. You gave Yourself for me."

That's the measuring stick. That is giving until it hurts. And until then, we don't know what it is to say, "I gave until it hurt."

I'm asking you today, be a person of faith, do your absolute best for God.

Give until it hurts today. Give your life. Crucified.

Learning How to Give Cheerfully

Remember our first chapter about 'Stuart?' Remember He had a room that we weren't allowed in? It was small. Only ten percent of the entire ship. That ten percent contained His money.

There is a common misperception among Christians that we 'give God our tithes' in the offering place. What the Bible teaches is that we give God 'His tithe' and *our offerings beyond the ten percent.*

I don't know anyone that enjoys giving (paying) income taxes. Sure, it's the way that we support the many great things that our government helps provide for us. But it's still a big chunk of money for most people. And relative to the rest of the world, our portion in the USA is very small. But the facts remain; somewhere between about 25% to 55% of the money we earn *is not ours and is allocated for someone else.*

The Biblical perspective of a 'tithe' is similar to a 'tax.' (Without all the pain, the paperwork, the fines and hassles!) One significant difference; *taxes are mandatory.*

Paying the tithe it is not mandatory. However, **giving it is a reflection of your character and response to His grace.** As the government so nicely swipes away your hard-earned money from the top of your pay check, consider wilfully, intentionally, joyfully setting also the top 10% of your net, (or better yet, the gross income), for the Lord's purposes. That's right: before the bills, expenses, and entertainment.

Be sure to not violate the standard that 'Stuart' put in place. If you venture into *his room* and *spend his money (the tithe)* this would demonstrate a poor stewardship decision. And stewards are concerned with being wise and protecting assets for the owner.

Also, do not include using the tithe in your monthly family expenses. Sure, put the tithe in your budget. But allocated funds just like it's an expense. Don't use Stuart's money to pay bills. Make your budget on the net assets you have *after* the tithe and taxes. Then, you will have a more realistic budget and keep yourself from getting into debt. That way, it is done and out of the way. Then, carefully decide to where you will invest the tithe.

The primary responsibility is first to your local church, and second to ministries that are doing the Lord's work. Remember, the people who set aside the first fruits of their resources to God are dedicating themselves to God, and not themselves to themselves.

A proper understanding of stewardship helps us realize that we are not the owner (King) of the resources we are charged with overseeing. Stewardship it is not designed to make us look good, but to make God look good. It forces us to think clearly of who we are in Christ.

Proper stewardship is recognizing our gifts and abilities as well as *opportunities,* then carrying out the responsibility of their care. It is also cooperation with other good stewards and helps us work as a team.

Stewardship is a tangible, measurable way for us to recognize the amazing wonder and power of grace that we did not deserve.

Stewardship forces us to be honest, and not rationalizing dishonesty for personal or even Kingdom gain. We are thankful for His gift of grace and would never want to violate our love of Christ.

Stewardship is not hording resources (money) for our comfort, because He is our source comfort. It is to make sure that we don't covet what others have, even if we can rationalize it for Kingdom gain.

Stewardship is just as important in taking care of the small things, because they are as important as the big things.

Stewardship is not lazy and seeking for the easy way out of work. Instead, stewardship is alert, active and looks a lot like working hard.

Proper stewardship is making sure that we don't fall in love with and worship the things we are supposed to care for, *while we forsake the One who gave it to us in the first place. It is not material things that are evil; it is what we do with them (and that they do to us) that is in violation of God's character. Anything that violates His character is evil, according to the Biblical perspective.* Money, in and of itself, is not evil; it is the abuse of money that is evil.

Stewardship is not being cheap and selfish. It is not 'pinching pennies' so we save a little, while we waste much more. Proper stewardship blesses those who serve us instead of holding onto coins making us 'penny wise and pound foolish.'

Stewardship brings a proper focus and attention on Christ. It glorifies Him with our care for His resources.

Stewardship realizes and recognizes that our giving is incredible minute compared to the endless blessings he has given to us.

A Proper understanding of stewardship means that we *know that if we obey we will be blessed for it.*

Stewardship means that we are not working to cover up our sins, but confessing, and repenting.

Stewardship is a humble spiritual position and it will allow us to let God be our leader and teacher.

Stewardship helps us realize that we are in community with those around us. In this process, we should exercise sound judgment and encouragement.

Stewardship absolutely puts us in a position to trust God, who provides for our spiritual and physical needs.

Stewardship sees our financial support of Kingdom ministries (tithing) as an investment. It pays the dividends with eternal values in mind. It is not a burden because of theloss of temporary goods.

Stewardship requires the sacrifice of our will, which is a spiritual maturity process.

Stewardship helps us honor our faith and social relationships and we are honoring the people around us.

Stewardship is part of our "prospering." It is an indication of our maturity and relationship with Christ.

This perspective will also allow you to give more easily and continually. We will look more at this in the following scriptures.

Read Hebrews 6:10; 13:16

1. Have you ever received a reward or a prize for an accomplishment? How did that make you feel? How do you feel knowing, as a person of faith, you will be rewarded by Christ Himself?

2. How can knowing that the faithful will be rewarded and the unfaithful will be damned help *you to have more confidence in your growth and service?*

3. The Bible teaches that those who are in Christ will receive blessings, and those who willfully reject Him will be cursed. Is this fair? Yes or no? Why?

4. At His second coming, Jesus will be looking for those who are prepared and faithful. What have you learned to help you be prepared? How does Stewardship help? Explain.

5. Why is it never in vain when we serve God and when we give?

6. How does it make you feel that when you give, to know that it is never forgotten by the One Who counts?

7. Why is God pleased when we make a personal sacrifice?

8. Why do most people (including some Christians) find it difficult to make a personal sacrifice?

9. What can you do to be a person who demonstrates wisdhom for the resources he has provided?

10. Explain how stewardship pleases God.

11. Explain how stewardship is worshipping God.

12. How does poor management and oversight of God's resources hinder our potential growth or increase in resources in the future?

13. When you look at your resources, what do you give and what is the source of the blessing?

14. Is your faith a 'daring' kind of faith? Is there something that you could learn or understand about stewardship that would help you move forward in your faith?

Remind yourself:
My Purpose Is:

What Belongs to Me?

Stewardship requires that we look after everything that God has provided to us in His world. We have to be diligent, honest and faithful, just like the character of God. With all of the Bible's concepts, precepts and principles, how are we supposed to manage all of this stuff?

Look at stewardship as a loan. We are given the responsibility (which means someone will check up on us at some point) to manage it with the attitude that at some point, we will return it to God. We should work to 'make Him proud' (honor) just like the Parable of the Talents demonstrates (Matthew 25:14-30).

It's important that you and I understand the difference between what 'we' have and what 'God' has. It's actually pretty simple.

We basically have nothing; we own nothing, earn nothing and we will gain nothing.

God on the other hand, is the actual (true) owner of everything. He owns it all.

Imagine this: when you die, the pall bearers will back up a trailer will all of your 'stuff' and bury it with you. Do you think that when you get to Heaven that there will be a team of people ready to help you move into your mansion on the golden streets with all of that 'stuff?' I would suggest that it is highly unlikely. It will all be buried right beside you where anyone could dig it up years later.

Besides, your 'eternal reward' is far superior to anything you could take with you. Even if you were a billionaire, your money wouldn't buy anything in heaven and you wouldn't even want it. It's hard to imagine, but you wouldn't even *need it.*

What God has in store for you is *far better than anything you could take with you! All we could bring would end up in the trash bins in Heaven!* That's all because of God's grace! (Deuteronomy 8:18; Psalm 24:1; Haggai 2:8; 1 Corinthians 6:16-20)!

Did you know that the Egyptians believed that they could take it with them. How do we know they were wrong? Because if you go to the Museums in Cairo you will see all of their grand stuff still there, here on earth!

We have to see this life as a dress rehearsal for the next life. We are given things: property, material possessions, gifts, ability, and most importantly, relationships with people. How we handle these things and what we learn from them, as well as how we impact others that becomes the *true treasure we are laying up in Heaven.*

It is not our mortgage deeds, auto titles, bank and investment statements or our retirement accounts that matter. *It is that we do with what is **temporarily given to us that matters. This is where the 'treasure' that Christ taught about is 'earned and learned.'***

God is the owner of all things. We are the managers, the overseers, the stewards, of those things placed in our care.

Take time to use and manage His resources wisely, realizing it is to prepare us for what is still on its way. (Psalm 49:16-17; Matthew 16:27; 25:21-23; Luke 19:12-19; 1 Corinthians 6:3; 2 Corinthians 4:16- 5:10; Revelation 20:6).

Think about this: when we 'sacrifice' and 'give' we are *actually giving resources that are not ours to begin with. We are giving **back to God what is already His.** It is not ours to keep, nor is it something we would even want to (or could) bring to eternity.*

So, we give what we cannot keep TO GAIN what we cannot lose!

This is authentic stewardship in action, and the real practicing of our faith. It is the practicing of our faith that is inseparable to the exercise of what we are given. These two combine synergistically to build our maturity and our standing before our Lord.

Its impossible to build your faith while ignoring your personal responsibilities. And you cannot build your faith by just focusing on material goods, even if you 'have a good heart' and you are doing these things faithfully. You just can't have one side of the equation. You get them both.

What about the stuff? What about our overflowing garages, attics and closets? What about those storehouses we pay for each month to house our extra things?

Well, material things are not wrong when viewed rightly. It is when we think of them as "important" (more important that God) that is considered foolish in God's eyes (Proverbs 23:5; Matthew 6:19-21; 19:21- 30).

1. How do our feelings about money become contrary to God's precepts? Why will they lead us to destruction? What can you do about it?

2. Have you seen in others (or experienced for yourself) the lesson that when we just live to acquire 'more stuff' that we actually end up with nothing of real consequence? How so?

3. How can you seek God, His perspective and His wisdom to give you greater understanding, skill, trust, hope, security, and opportunities?

Read Proverbs 20:10; 22:7; Luke 12:15; 16: 10-11; Ephesians 4:28; 1 Timothy 6:10

Dig deep: Why is money important to you?

Why do you think it is important to God? How is it important to the Lord?

Read 2 Corinthians 9:6-15: What does the Scripture outline as the principles of giving?

Read Mark 12: 41-44; Romans 12:10; 1 Corinthians 3:16-17; 6:19-20; 3 John 2

Looking at those texts, what does it mean to you that God considers you His temple?

With that 'picture' in mind, how are you going to respond differently to Him, and with the time, treasures, and talent in your life?

What about your health? How can you take better control and care of your body? Read Psalm 50: 14-15; Proverbs 22:9, 28:13; Job 36:11; Isaiah. 48:17; Luke 6:38; Philippians 4:19

List some of God's promises regarding stewardship.

"The time you invest in the quiet will benefit you in the storm' someone said. Take some time: settle in. Spend some quality time in "surrendered" prayer; that is, pray with your will and desires set aside so you can listen to God and His wonderful plan for you!

Prayerfully decide on how you plan to implement God's desires and call to be a better steward of all the relationships, time, talent, money, and resources in your life!

Remind yourself again:
        What is my purpose?

Just Exactly What is a Tithe?

Most of us have been taught that the giving of one tenth of our gross financial income to our local church is 'tithing.' That sounds fine and good. But again, it's not what we think that counts. It's what the Bible teaches that matters. Let's look at it.

I know it sounds weird to say this, but *nowhere in the New Testament does it advocate tithing. And the Old Testament only has two narrative passages on this subject, along with scores of other texts that are usually taken out of context which is why there is so much confusion on this topic.*

We should always be careful to not build 'doctrines' (spiritual faith absolutes) on narratives or stories from the Bible. This is because stories (like those about Abraham and Melchizedek) do not necessarily represent the Godly character or doctrines *we are supposed to follow. Sometimes they do and sometimes they don't. A 'doctrinal' position doesn't have 'sometimes' in its formula. A doctine "always does" and "never does" but never 'sometimes.'*

Consider the 'story' of David and Bathsheba. It's story with a spiritual component. However, just because David had an affair does not mean that it's okay for us to have an affair, right? This historical story is about David's heart, his actions; the good, bad and the ugly. So be careful how you interpret Scripture; just because it's "in" the Bible does not mean that it's okay. After all, the Bible has murders, affairs, lying, deceit and stories of numerous sins throughout. That does not mean that those things are okay for us as Children of God.

Stewardship, however, is a different subject. Throughout the Bible, the principles and guidelines for stewardship never change. The Bible is clear and it admonishes us to be good stewards, especially in the handling of our money, and it gives us a roadmap for action (1 Corinthians 9:7).

Here are the Scriptures from the Old Testament.

Personal offerings:

Abraham paid tithes to Melchizedek, and tithes of a tenth of 'the heap,' which he took from the kings with whom he fought in battle (Gen. 14:20; Heb. 7:2-6).

When Jacob made his covenant with God at Bethel, he also made a vow, and gave a tenth of all his property to God (Gen. 28:16-22).

Samuel warned Israel that the king whom they were demanding from God, would exact tithes of their grain and flocks (I Sam. 8:10-18).

There are more examples of free-will offerings found in Gen. 4:1-7; 8:20; Ex. 25:35-36; Deut. 12:6; 16:10-17; 1 Chron. 29:1-17; and Heb. 7:4-10).

Tithe Offerings:

Mosaic laws instructing the Jews how to provide for the nation and church/Temple Duet. 26:12-15.

The First Fruits offering: Ex. 23:16-19; 34:22-26; Lev. 2:12-14; 23:10- 20; Num. 18:12; 28:26; Deut. 26:10; 2 Kings 4:42; 2 Chron. 31:5; Neh. 10:35-37; 12:44; 13:31; Prov. 3:9-10

The Levites' Tithe for the priests: Lev. 27:30-33; Num. 18:21-29; Deut. 12:6-18; 14:22-29; Neh. 10:38: 18:21; Heb. 7:5

Temple Tax: Ex. 30:11-16; Neh. 10:32-39; 2 Chron. 31:11-12; Mal. 3:10; 12:44; 13:5, 12; Matt. 17:24-27

Sabbath Tax: Ex. 23:10-11; Deut. 15:1-9

The Poor Tithe: Deut. 14:28-29

Farmers' Tax: (leaving crops un-harvested for the poor) Lev. 19:9-10; Deut. 24:19-21: Ruth 2.

Principles on Stewardship and Tithing:
Cultural customs relating to: Neh. 10:37-38; Amos 4:4; Heb. 7:5-9.

The tithe was also a form of worship and dedication to the Lord: Deut. 26:12f.

The New Testament Tithe principles: 2 Cor. 8:12-15; Matt. 23:8-10; 23; Luke 18:12' Heb. 7:8-9.

The New Testament Stewardship principles: Matt. 6: 19-34; 19:21; Mark 12:41-44; Luke 6:38; 12:15; 33; 16:11-12; 19:1-10; 21:1-4; Rom 12:6; 10; 1 Cor. 4:1-2; 8:8-15; 9:7; 6:19-20; 2 Cor. 9:6-15; Eph. 4:28; Phil. 4:19; 5:15-16; 1 Tim. 6:10; James 1:17; 3 John 2).

The example of the early church: Acts 2:43-47; 4:32-5:11; 11:27-30; 20:35; Rom. 15:22-29; 1 Cor. 16:1-4; 2 Cor. 8-9; Phil. 4:14-19; 1 Tim. 6:6-19; Heb. 13:16.

Historically, this is what the Jewish household was required to do:

The Jewish household was obligated to share ten percent of their income, *(in whatever form)* that would fulfill the Levites' tithe (Lev. 27:30- 32; Deut. 14:22-23; Num. 18:21).

Every Jewish household was obligated to make a declaration of honesty before the Lord with their giving (Deut 26:13-15). The Temple was the place to which tithes were taken (Deut. 12:5-17).

There was a fine of twenty percent that had to be paid if they withheld or refused to pay what was required, in the form that was required, such as if they were required to give a sheep and they gave coins instead. Or, an extra tithe, a fifth of the sum, was demanded from those who sold their tithes. So, if you were required to give a sheep, but you sold it to your neighbor, and then refused to use the money to pay for a substitute (Lev. 27:31-33).

The Levites, in turn, gave a tenth of their share (not all of the Levites were priests, as some served as government officials) to provide for the priests (Num. 18:25-32).

Historically, the tithe was gathered once a year, and then an extra tithe was gathered every third year for those in need locally (Deut. 14:22-28). (Not every Hebrew scholar agrees with this, as some say this only happened when the need for funds increased because of the building and expansion of the Temple.)

Then over time, mankind being the selfish beings we are, the folks in charge would overtax the people, adding extras that were not required by God, but by man's greed (recorded in the Talmud, an ancient Jewish commentary).

The Jews tithed (paid taxes) to their government, whether Babylonian, Roman or whoever were the invading rulers at the time (again a historical reference). Sometimes, evil kings took over and hoarded the funds for themselves, such as Manasseh. At other times, tithes were withheld (2 Kings 18; Neh. 13:10; Mal. 3:8). Tithes resumed in Hezekiah's reign (2 Chron. 31:5-10) and under Nehemiah (Neh. 13:12).

There were extra sacrificial offerings sometimes required (2 Sam. 6; 1 Kings 6-8; 12: 25-33; 2 Chron. 31:5-12; Ezek. 45:17; Amos: 7:13; Luke 18:12)

Then there was this: The payment of an extra governing tithe/tax, as Samuel had warned would happen, and then was practiced (1 Sam. 8:15-17). Sounds like modern day politics!

By the time Jesus arrived, the Romans and "over-eager tax gatherers" greatly affected the economic life of the Jews; so, most were unable to tithe to the Temple. However, the laws regarding the tithe were still observed as shown here by Jesus (Matt 23:23; Luke 11:42).

1. How what is your attitude about Stewardship now? What has changed?

2. How important are *your perspectives* and viewpoints on life? Are you confident that you are right? How so? What would it take for you to change your viewpoint on a particular subject, such as something so personal as stewardship?

3. What are some things you have done which you feel demonstrate your sincerity and heart?

4. Re-read all that the Jewish household was required to do. How does this impact you and your understanding of God and His plan?

5. When we realize who we are in Christ, all of our problems and opportunities come into perspective. How has this been so for you?

6. How can you seek God, His perspective, and His wisdom to give you greater understanding, skills, trust, hope, security, and opportunities?

7. How does being "self-focused" prevent you from gaining anything of real value?

8. Do you believe that wealth is *never* evidence of God's work or blessings?

9. Do you believe that we are made rich in who we are in Christ, not in our circumstances? Why, then, do many Christians think otherwise?

10. How does your *ability* to be a Christian (who realizes that you are the witness to the Light of Christ) become the light that impacts others?

11. Do you realize that your *reliability,* in being a light to those who are weak in Him or do not know Him, will be the essence of Christ they may see in you (John 1:6-9; 1 John 1:7)?

12. What can your church do to influence its people to be better stewards?

Here are more key verses for your consideration: 2 Chronicles 31:5-12; Nehemiah 10:37-38; Amos 4:4; Malachi 3:8-10.

Multiple Tithes Hurt

For the most part, it is hard to give a precise reconstruction of a typical tithe from the Old Testament. One reason is that over time the practice changed, from the desert wandering under Moses, to the period of the Judges, then the Kings, the captivities, the different localities of Judea vs. Israel, local governments, and invading governments. In addition, there was abuse by the Pharisees (they were not "fair, you see") and other leaders in charge by over-taxing. However, from Scripture, we do know what was required.

First, every year, a Jewish household gave ten percent of all of their goods or produce; this was the "Levite's Tithe." Historically, The Levites did not have land as the rest of the twelve tribes did. (Joseph's cut was split in two with Ephraim and Manasseh to make twelve). So, the rest of the tribes were called to support the Levites. (The Levites were the priests). This was the tax to the government that funded the office of the priesthood. Remember, Israel was a theocracy, a government run by the Church, or in their case, the priests, the Judges, and then the Kings, all of whom were under God. The countless thousands of priests were the teachers, rabbis/pastors, and government officials.

It would be like if today, the Mayor, Governor, Senate, and Congress did not represent the people by vote. Since (the rules are) all spelled out in the Law, they only sought the Will of God by examining the Scriptures. God told them what to do. So the tithe was also supporting the running of the government. I would offer the perspective that it is safe to say that we do not live in a theocracy today.

Second, the Jewish household would give *another* ten percent every year for the festivals and the religious sacrifices. (This is what the people were doing by dropping in coins, or bringing animals to the Temple when Jesus was there teaching. Because the leaders abused the system by selling what they were not supposed to, Jesus drove them out with a whip!) So, the running of the Temple/church, Sabbaths, holy days, and each one's personal offering to God accounted for ten percent (the literal percentage, the exact amount and how often this was practiced is a matter of debate).

Third, the Jewish household would pay *another* ten percent every third year to the poor and the widows locally (again the percentage, exact amount and how often this was practiced is a matter of debate).

So, if you were an OT Jew, you *definitely* would pay ten percent of your income, in whatever form was required to the Levites and/or the local government, to support them and the operation of the priests, Temple, and government. Then you could pay (depending on where you were in history) *another* ten percent to provide for the Temple, festivals, and such, plus your personal sacrifice for atonement. Then, you might be required to pay *another* ten percent every third year for the needy. **Is anybody counting all those ten percents? That's 30% every third year, with no deductions, Earned Income Child Deductions or charitable giving!**

What does this all mean? Well, if you claim a "tithe" is *just ten percent,* you would be incorrect. That's because there were several tithes plus freewill offerings! Also, there was the shekel temple tax, and the tax that was required if they were occupied by a foreign power (They were occupied by the Romans, but the government was not run by the Romans. This is why Jesus said, "Render to Caesar the things that are Caesar's." In other words, pay the Romans what they ask for, and render to God the things that are required by God).

As if this wasn't enough, if you were a farmer, you were *required* to leave about ten percent of your crop *un-harvested,* for the poor. The farmers would have square fields and would harvest in a circle, leaving the corners for feeding the poor.

The actual breakdown of the entire "tithe" load was around **23.3%** per year, *plus* the atonement offerings, to which most Jewish scholars say the total could have been as high as *thirty to forty percent* **plus** *foreign taxes.* Again, scholars debate the exact percentage, amount, and how often this was practiced, but you get the picture. It was far more than ten percent!

Isn't it interesting that the base tax system in the United States is about twenty to thirty percent. When you add income tax and the various sales taxes, we pay about twenty-five percent! *But, this does not include the tithe to God, who says, "Let every man bring whatever he purposes in his heart; let him do it willingly, whatever he wants to give."*

In the book of Acts, we find that they kept bringing so much in that they had to say, "Stop, don't bring anymore-- that's enough." So, if we did pay ten percent of our net salary to the church, we would be paying generally the same percentage as the Israelites were called to do. *Remember that giving is always a freewill offering, coming from what is in our heart. It is an expression of our gratitude, worship, and love to our Lord!* So, do whatever you want to do from this perspective. Exercise the "good heart" that you have. But, be on guard and do not allow your pride and greed to cloud your reasoning and call!

"Rejoice in the Lord always. I will say it again: Rejoice! Let your gentleness be evident to all. The Lord is near. Do not be anxious about anything, but in everything, by prayer and petition, with thanksgiving, present your requests to God. And the peace of God, which transcends all understanding, will guard your hearts and your minds in Christ Jesus" (Philippians 4:4-7).

1. Do you have a better (different) understanding of what a tithe is?

2. What do you think were **God's** motivations and desires for the Jewish people regarding tithing?

3. How can you have an attitude to "Rejoice in the Lord always" in your Tithing and giving?

4. Can you explain the Levite's Tithe? How is this like the modern day church?

5. Does understanding the history and biblical roots of a tithe help you manage your money and resources today?

6. Do you see wealth as a good thing or bad thing? Is there a balanced view? Is wealth "the" sign of God's blessings? Why, or why not?

7. Why do you think that God says He will not ignore the poor? Do you hear their cries? What can you do to be a better steward of caring for the poor?

8. How can you have your mind *ready to learn and grow* from your experiences?

9. How can healthy stewardship become more of a regular, normal, and daily part of your life?

10. When you look at the Scriptures, Jesus obviously calls us to be radical in our service **and** mature in our attitude and faith. It's not either or…it's 'both and.' What does this mean to you?

11. What do you think God wants you to do your giving?

12. What is a biblical, healthy and responsible way your church can teach its people about Tithing?

Remind yourself:
    What is my purpose?

Is Tithing For the Modern Day Believer?

"All the Church wants me for is my money."

"The Church is always asking for money."

"I never know what my Church is doing with all that money."

It's enough to make you head explode. The oversight and care for money is a real temperature gauge to measure someone's character. It's right out there in the open. It's hard to miss. We all know the pain that comes from the mismanagement of government (a non-profit) funds or relief funds. It's seems like its always a 'sad ending.'

One reason that 'the Church' has to *ask* for money is that many people run away from stewardship because they do not see it as God does. Sadly, this is an indication of our spiritual condition!

We should not, and cannot, ever separate money and finances from our spiritual life.

Yet, some Christians do, hoping to be satisfied with what they can keep, not with how their resources can be used for the Kingdom.

Have you ever thought that the way we give is a snapshot of what is in our hearts and our level of commitment to our Lord? And, when we refuse to give or are very stingy, *we are missing key opportunities to serve and be used of God?*

If we really want to be mature and growing Christians, we must take the Bible seriously. We just have to. This means that we work at discovering God's character, respecting His holiness, develop a healthy fear (respect) of Him, and have a sense of awe, while learning how we can grow in our faith.

When we realize (and admit) what Christ did for us, we can start to take to heart the seriousness of being a wise steward.

Stewardship is an act of worship and gratitude by the Believer, in response to His grace. In so doing, we acknowledge God's power and authority over our lives. Then, we respond to others around us with these godly precepts.

Want to start a discussion with some 'high blood pressure" at your next small group meeting? All you have to do is bring up stewardship and tithing. The old religious emotions will run hot, guaranteed. In fact, to make things 'saucy' be sure to make it a debate and you will have a great time. You might not win any friends, but you will have lively discussion.

Stewardship and tithing are 'hot topics' and Christians seem to love the banter and debate. However, many (can I say most?) have a skewed idea and understanding what these subjects are really all about. Most of the conversation will be based upon "Well I think" as opposed to "God's Word says…" kinds of insight. These assumptions aren't always in line with God's Word and that's a really dangerous place to be.

I know that it is essential to form an argument on facts and logic, and not emotionalism and presumptions. With Scripture, this is fundamental and critical. The Bible is not a menu, where we can pick and choose what would fit our experiences and preferences, ignoring the rest, and being unconcerned with what God's Word really said in its simple and concise form. This is for sure: The Bible means what it says and says what it means. The key is context: not adding what is not there, or removing what is there.

One theme seems to surface whenever we talk about stewardship. People do not want to take responsibility for what God's Word says, or what stewardship really means in applying it to their wallets.

Emotions and our individual, personal wills block reason and the truth of Scripture. Carefully crafted arguments, justification for disobedience, and people tangling up the Word to "support" their views, all designed so they did not have to give to the church.

This is a sad place to be. It's a disastrous place to stay.

1. Looking back on your life, what happens when all a person does is chase wealth?

2. How would you say that being a good steward gives you a sense of victory, hope, and comfort?

3. How have you had some 'interesting' discussions with other believers about tithing? How often are the points from Scripture and from personal feelings? Why does this matter?

4. Do you agree that most Christians today have a skewed idea of what stewardship? Why is that? Is it based on their assumptions, not the facts from God's Word?

5. How would you say that your life has been affected by your 'desire' for money? How has money become a way for you to measure worth for you or for others whom you have known?

6. What have you learned from these Scriptures that we have been studying about being responsible?

7. Would you say that you are chasing your desires or Jesus? How does this answer compare to your written purpose?

8. Describe your perspective on life; what is God doing in you and through you?

9. Looking back on your life, do you see good times or bad times as more important? Which is more influential?

10. What do you need to do so that you can focus on how you can be more obedient with His call to the poor and oppressed?

11. How does our love and kindness show us the possibilities and opportunities Jesus gives us? What happens when we do not do this?

12. One of the aspects of life in Christ is that He gives us the ability to learn and grow through good financial gains and your tough money days? How can it better keep you from stress and worry?

13. How does the pursuit of wealth rob ourselves of Christ Himself being our substance to meet our needs?

14. Every life has 'good things' and 'bad things' moving in and out of daily life. How can you handle it (good or bad) with excellence and learn and grow from it? How would your walk with Christ grow and in turn be a blessing to others if you did this?

A growing, mature Christian realizes their responsibility of stewardship in all things. They may even struggle in prayer over the issue and even with family with regard as what to give. But going back to God's Word, they will discover how they can serve God and the local church. They don't rationalize that it is not profitable, it's not good, to ignore the call of God, to refrain from using their gifts and talents, to refuse to share their faith or to withhold their financial resources. As people saved by grace, *we should be overwhelmed with gratitude for what Christ has done for us* **so that we naturally desire to serve Him with all of our hearts and all of our means.**

Yes, it's true. You are not 'forced' to do anything because we are saved by faith alone. However, our faith demands action (James 1).

Once we have grown into a life of maturity, we find a strong sene of gratitude for God's grace. This prompts us to do something about our stewardship. It makes us aware that we have to take care of all that He has given to us.

How do we respond
    How much do we keep
        How much do we give
            How much is for our pleasure
                How much is for the Kingdom

There are no simple, solid answers here. They differ for everyone. It truly is a heart matter. It's a *response of our heart and faith.*

We are given some basic guidelines from Scripture: but it is up to us to figure out how to apply them *to our lives.*

It seems that there is an attitude 'hitting the pew' (or in my case, the padded chair) that if God loves a "cheerful giver" (2nd Corinthians 9:7) that we only have to tithe whatever makes us 'cheerful.' That could be two, five, ten percent or none. Believe it or not, there are those who interpret these thoughts and behaviors to mean that *if they don't resent the amount they are tithing,* **as long as they are cheerful about it, remaining happy, content and generous about whatever they 'tithe' then they can say they are cheerful.**

I don't think I need to tell you that I don't think that is what God had in mind. But then again, I just told you that I don't think that is what God had in mind.

Since it all comes from Him, and belongs to Him, we are cheerful and grateful for His underlying gift of grace and our giving is a response to His kindness. *Being cheerful is being focused on what he has done for us.*

So many countries, governments and agencies require a lot more from us than God does. He allows us to use 90% of the resources. He asks us to acknowledge His Sovereignty by physically giving back (it's already His!) 10% *for our benefit.*

The idea and structure of giving what is comfortable is directly contrary to Scripture. It's convenient. But contrary.

We may not be required to give an exact amount or percentage, since we are under grace and not law as the Puritans argued, but they gave way more than a mere ten percent! So, look at this verse in its context (2 Cor. 9:6- 15), especially verse six, and you will see that this popular thinking is wrong! This passage is an illustration from farming (Job. 4:8; Prov. 11:18; 22:8; Hos. 8:7; 10:12). Thus, when you give, your gift will be used as a seed that grows into a crop.

I don't know any other investment that can do this. The more you give to the Kingdom, the more results there will be in the Kingdom. Both the giving of the gift *and the maturity of the person who gives*, will grow. This is what Paul calls "sufficiency" which means to be content in all circumstances. The opposite would be to be self-sufficient. If you would like to read about it, the book of Jeremiah tells us how much God hates that! So we strive to see the beauty of giving and be cheerfully motivated.

Keep in mind that being a cheerful giver is about responding to God, not to our conveniences.

Also, our giving is nothing compared to the gift of grace we have been given (John 3:16)!

We will actually end up robbing God when we refuse to give, or give too little. The most important investment we could ever make is in the Kingdom of God (Mal. 3: 8).

Remember, we don't' just tithe on our money; it is our time, treasure, and talent. So, we give our time, gifts, and abilities of commitment and service to our Lord, and to His Church.

We must remain aware that our fallen, human depravity will get in the way and rationalize our behaviors that we want to do over the call of the God!

1. Ask yourself: What does it mean to you that God loves a cheerful giver? How can giving away our possessions, resources, money and time be fun and cheerful?

2. Have you ever considered that when we just chase "stuff" all we end up doing is robbing ourselves of the riches that God has to give us? How and why are these worthless and meaningless?

3. Would you say that most Christians give out of our conveniences? How have you seen or done this? How is this in direct opposition to what Scripture says?

4. How does responding to God (not our conveniences) help us become a cheerful giver? How does this happen?

5. Do you realize that your giving, (no matter how grand) is no comparison to the gift of grace you have been given? How does that motivate you?

6. Once we form a more mature faith, and develop a strong sense of gratitude for the grace flowing in us, how does that impact our level of stewardship?

9. What does it mean to show the attitude and conduct of Christ? What would that look like in your life?

10. Is this true? If you cannot handle what God has trust you with now, how can you manage more of what He may give in the future?

11. How you deal with stewardship will show your true character, maturity, and spiritual growth. True or False?

12. How you deal with financial problems can make your situation positive and meaningful. How so? If not, what is in the way?

The early church prescribed a tithe for all of its members who were able to pay. They saw ten percent owed to God as the ***absolute minimum*** from a person's total income, the least anyone should be able to do. Even Monks had to pay.

Later on in Church history, it was believed (and practiced) that a follower of Christ was to live the most modest life possible, sell his possessions, and give to the poor based on the passage in Matthew (Matt. 19:21; Gal. 5:1).

They saw tithing as law, *but we were not under law.* In addition, they believed that since everything belonged to God, we should just give Him everything. By the time of legal Christianity, the ideas of tithing had changed so much that the application of giving ten percent was accepted and practiced in all the provinces and nations that were Christian. By the Eighth Century, the Holy Roman Empire took over and the tithe became the tax to Rome, in addition to any governing tax. In the twelfth century, the Monks got a reprieve, so, not only did they not have to pay tithes, they also were able to receive them (before it became the obligation of families to care for them).

At this time, controversies over what a tithe is, how much the Christian was to give and the Church was to receive, was highly intense. The main opponents to tithing were those who did not want to give versus those who did; between those who wanted the tithe for themselves versus those who did not want their money wasted on corruption. By the Middle Ages, tithes had become as complicated as those in Jesus' day. With specific regulations, twisted out of the context of the Scripture and levied on the poor, such as tithes to the church, the priests, vicars, and personal tithes-- were extracted from their produce, for which each category had different regulations (just like our IRS tax code today), different from hay, to corn, to wood, to monies.

Then in the pre-reformation, intense conflict arose with tithing; it then escalated during the Reformation. Just a generation after the Reformation, more controversy arose, especially in England where there was a state church.

This escalated into the English Civil War. What was the issue and why there was a civil war? A whole county fought over tithing! This was one of the reasons that led the Puritans to flee. The Puritans desired the tithe to be voluntary and not mandatory, just as Scripture prescribes. The state tithe in England lasted up until a few decades ago-- to support the state church!

Consider this. Without faithful giving, we would have no way to finance the spread of the gospel, missions, evangelism, social programs, kids and youth programs, or even the building of the Church. Not just the buildings, but the people, programs, and opportunities to do as our Lord has called us to do would suffer! We could not impact our neighbourhoods with His love, or minister to the needs of men. Yet, our neighbourhoods are suffering from violence, the breakdown of the family, juvenile delinquency, substance abuse--the list goes on--while most of the neighbourhood churches sit, doing little to nothing. There is no vision, no programs, all because of one thing that is missing--no money!

Here is something else to consider. The "smart" economists say that if we removed the nation's income tax system and went to a "flat rate" of ten percent across the board for everything, our US National budget will be plentiful--and balanced! All we would have to do is divide ten percent from the gross national product, com- pare it to what the IRS gets annually, and what the national debt is. But, we probably will not see this happen due to political jockeying; it is too simple, and it would work. The rich would pay more because they buy more. The poor would pay less, and so forth. It would be a level playing field. The tithe is on the same level playing/paying field, too. It was, when first instituted, and it is still fair today. Everyone is at the same standard; there are no favourites.

Is Tithing for Today? The answer is no--as a forced obligation.

The answer is also yes--if it is a response from the heart. We are not *obligated* to give any amount, minimum or maximum. Jesus told one man to give half of what he had. He told another man to give everything. Tithing is a heart issue. When we have the right mindset, based on the Word of God and a heart that flows with gratitude for what He has done, yes, *we will want to give all that we are able to.*

I believe that in the debates, occurring over the centuries since the early church, and now to the classrooms in seminary, money and religion have always gone together. Money and religion have always fought each other in people's pride and inclinations. Jesus was upset with "money changers." Martin Luther's was outraged with the selling of indulgences in the pre-Reformation period. Television (and local) preachers have been known to say something like, "If you give to me, God will give to you ten times as much." Problem is, that's really bad math and investment advice. In the end, it all comes down to motivation, greed, and the idol of money. We will bow to money or we will bow to God. The question is what do you truly worship? Where is your motivation? Where is your heart?

Find ways to be "Investing in Futures." Your future. Your family's future. Your Church's future. The Kingdom's future. You will find the experience rewarding, enriching and satisfying. When it comes to finances, no other area of life comes with the challenge and reward of managing our finances God's way. When God is honored, God blesses. When God blesses, it flows in abundance.

1. Do you worry about money? What can meet your financial needs? How can the worship of our Lord replace your worry? What can you do to get in a state of worship when worry comes your way?

2. Would you say that Tithing is for Today? Why, why not what will you do?

3. What do you need to do to focus on how you can be more obedient with His call to the poor and oppressed?

4. How do money, sex, and power have an influence on you? What about in your church?

5. How can you be sure that money (stewardship), sex (good marital relationships) and power (positive influence and encouragement) are tools for His glory? What will be the real values in your life that will echo throughout eternity?

6. How can you put yourself in Jesus' hands, to be more of a person of faith and integrity?

7. How can you be one who is surrendered and poured out to Christ and used powerfully in the lives of others (John 3:30; Gal. 2:20-21; Phil. 3:10)?

8. How do you feel that without faithful giving, we would have no way to finance the spread of the gospel, missions, evangelism, social programs, kids and youth programs, or even the building of the Church?

9. How do you feel that people, programs, and opportunities will suffer and fail to do as our Lord has called us to do when we are disobedient in stewardship?

10. Are you chasing your desires or our Lord? How can the answer to this question help determine what direction you take in stewardship and honouring God?

11. How does our love and kindness show us the possibilities and opportunities Jesus gives us? What happens when we do not do this?

12. How is your attitude about Stewardship now? Have you realized yet that how you deal with stewardship will show your true character, maturity, and spiritual growth? Have you realized that how you deal with financial problems can make your situation positive and meaningful? How so? If not, what is in the way?

13. How can you have an attitude to Rejoice in the Lord always in your Tithing and giving?

Thanks for taking time to consider developing a healthy perspective on stewardship and tithing. Remember, to "Live On Purpose" means that your finances have to be aligned with your Purpose, as well.

God Bless You in your journey!

Dr. Tom Tufts &
The Family at Friends Community Church
Orlando, FL

Resources from

FRIENDS MEDIA GROUP

"LUDIO: Leadership Upside Down and Inside Out"
Study Guide/Small Group Discussion Book
Everyone is a leader! Leadership is most effective when it is done by serving people! And it's the most *fun* when you are leading from the heart! Paperback or E-Book $9.99

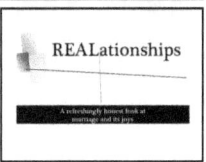
"REALationships: A Refreshingly Honest Look at Marriage and It's Joys" Rediscover *why* you got married and how to make it last! This is an in-depth, powerful series for individual couples and small group study. 6 week Workbook/Small Group Discussion Format Paperback or E-book $9.99

"Groomed For Success: Find Your Passion; Make it Your Mission"
What are the traits that make people a success? Find out how communication, perspiration, delegation and participation will take you on a journey toward personal fulfillment! Paperback and e-book $7.99

"eXtreme faith: life, love, faith and purity" Discover what it means to be a follower of Christ who lives a life of faith to the eXtreme! Easy to read, great stories and eXamples to impact your life! Paperback and e-book $7.99

Up for Grabs: Parenting in the 21st Century Times, they are 'a changing' as they say! Learn some simple principles and processes that can help you with your children. This book will help you understand *why they do what they do* and how you can help them become balanced, well-adjusted children. And you will be balanced, too! Paperback and e-book $7.99

Love You Love Notes
For Couples #1-100 To Her #1-100 To Him #1-100 To Kids #1-100
www.loveyoulovenotes.com

Also Check Out:

    For scheduling information for Dr. Tom Tufts
    www.tomtufts.com

For Additional Products:
    Shirts, Hats, Gear, Music CDs, Videos, Books, and more
    www.friendsmediagroup.com

Cover Designs: In Demand Speakers, Orlando, FL
    www.indemandspeakers.com

Back Cover Bio Picture: Xander Photography, Orlando, FL
    www.xanderphotos.com

Additional Notes:

Additional Notes:

Additional Notes: